CREATIVE ACCOUNTING – or How to make your profits what you want them to be – is essential reading for anyone involved in business and for all shareholders. This unexpurgated bible of the business world explodes the myth that profits are governed by a set of common principles and guidelines, showing how companies manipulate their reported results. Illustrated here with some of the most recent examples of corporate creativity are all the very latest schemes for: tampering with taxation, flattering the fixed assets, pilfering the pension fund and many other ways of cooking the books yet staying inside the law.

Ian Griffiths is a chartered accountant, who was educated at Wallasey Grammar School and Liverpool University. He is the Assistant News Editor on The Independent.

25 MAR. '89

CREATIVE ACCOUNTING

How to make your profits what you want them to be

IAN GRIFFITHS

UNWIN PAPERBACKS
London   Sydney

First published in Great Britain by Waterstone & Co Ltd in 1986
Reprinted by Sidgwick & Jackson Ltd 1987
First published in paperback by Unwin® Paperbacks, an imprint of Unwin
Hyman Limited, in 1987

UNWIN HYMAN LIMITED
Denmark House, 37–39 Queen Elizabeth Street, London SE1 2QB
and
40 Museum Street, London WC1A 1LU

Allen & Unwin Australia Pty Ltd
8 Napier Street, North Sydney, NSW 2060, Australia

Unwin Paperbacks New Zealand Pty Ltd with Port Nicholson Press
60 Cambridge Terrace, Wellington, New Zealand

British Library Cataloguing in Publication Data
Griffiths, Ian
Creative accounting: how to make your
profits what you want them to be.
1. Corporations—Great Britain—
Accounting
I. Title
657'.95'0941   HF5686.C7
ISBN 0–04–657003–9

Printed in Great Britain by
The Guernsey Press Co. Ltd., Guernsey, Channel Islands.

FOR MUM AND DAD

PREFACE

The use of creative accounting by companies to manipulate the figures reported in their annual accounts is widespread. This book highlights the main schemes which are currently in use. It will therefore be of assistance to those who prepare accounts. However, it should also provide some insight for shareholders and other users of financial information into the hidden techniques which are used in arriving at the numbers which are finally reported. There is no doubt that finance directors need the flexibility of creative accounting but by the same token the users of the finished product need to know how that flexibility has been implemented in practice. I hope this book goes some way towards bringing preparer and user closer together.

ACKNOWLEDGEMENTS

I am indebted to Paul Rutteman, a partner with accountants Arthur Young, who gave up his Christmas holiday to read through the manuscript. The value of his comments and observations is inestimable and I cannot thank him enough for his time and help.

My thanks also to Nigel Moore and Nigel MacDonald, partners in accountants Ernst and Whinney, for their ideas and assistance.

I should not ignore my former colleagues of *The Times Business News* who assisted in one form or another. In particular, I must single out Derek and Pam, who ensured that I did not overstay my welcome at the Calthorpe.

My special thanks, though, are reserved for Anne for her patience and encouragement throughout the project.

CONTENTS

1

AN INTRODUCTION to CREATIVE ACCOUNTING

*E*very company in the country is fiddling its profits. Every set of published accounts is based on books which have been gently cooked or completely roasted. The figures which are fed twice a year to the investing public have all been changed in order to protect the guilty. It is the biggest con trick since the Trojan horse.

Any accountant worth his salt will confirm that this is no wild assertion. There is no argument over the extent and existence of this corporate contortionism, the only dispute might be over the way in which it is described. Such phrases as 'cooking the books', 'fiddling the accounts' and 'corporate con trick' may raise eyebrows where they cause people to infer that there is something illegal about this pastime. In fact this deception is all in perfectly good taste. It is totally legitimate. It is creative accounting.

This above-the-board means of achieving underhand ends is rife in boardrooms throughout the country as companies contrive to translate their activities of the year into reported results which flatter the management and the share price. The methods which are used to manipulate the figures and the dramatic impact they have on a company's profits are described in detail in later chapters. They range from the very simple to the latest, highly sophisticated schemes which defy detection. Whatever the degree of complexity, the end result is always exactly the same. The company produces figures which are

1

only loosely based on fact.

The legacy for these rather crude adaptations of the year's events comes from the flexibility and vagueness of the accounting rules and company law which governs how financial statements should be prepared and presented. There is no black and no white, only grey. This country is blessed with a system of low definity monochrome accounting.

Yet no finance director can afford to be left behind in the creative accounting stakes. The opportunities to manipulate the profit and loss account, and the balance sheet which these schemes present, can no longer be overlooked. Financial information has become a propaganda weapon to be swung into action whenever the need arises. The days when a company's accounts were simply a record of its trading performance are long dead.

Having identified the financial statements, though, as the murder victim, and creative accounting as the murder weapon, all that is missing is the motive. The flat-footed sergeant turns to his inspector and asks, 'The only thing that puzzles me, chief, is why a company like that would want to do such a thing?'

The answer provides the key to creative accounting's growing popularity. The pressure on companies to report flattering results is greater than ever before. This necessity mothers the innovations in accounting creativity, which makes it increasingly difficult for users of financial information to discern fact from fiction.

Ironically, it is those users who have perhaps contributed most, directly and indirectly, to this climate of distortion. A combination of the increasing power of the big institutional investors and, at the same time, a move to encourage wider share ownership by small individual investors, has forced companies to tailor their results to meet more closely the demands of the stock market. Those demands dictate that a company produces a steady growth in profits and earnings and that it consistently lives up to the expectations imposed on it by an army of City analysts and research teams.

There is no doubt that a company which in four successive

years produces pre-tax profits of £1, £2, £4, and £8 million will be regarded in a better light than one which produces profits of £4 and £15 million in years one and three and pre-tax losses of £1 and £3 million in years two and four. The net profits for both companies in the period is exactly the same at £15 million. But the first company has a record which reveals profits doubling each year; while the second enterprise has a trading record which is erratic to say the least.

It may well be that the second company's results represent a more accurate reflection of the trading pattern of the business. Unfortunately, the stock market simply does not take kindly to such vagaries and much prefers the fantasy of smooth growth to the reality of fluctuating operational performance. It falls to the creative accountant to ensure that those fluctuations are removed by hoarding profits in the years of plenty for release in the years of famine.

But profits-smoothing is only one side-effect of this subtle influence imposed by the City. There is also the requirement for companies to live up to the market's expectations. These are generated by the analysts from the big stockbroking houses who forecast the profits from a particular company and then use these projections as the basis for persuading clients to buy or sell the shares. It is not hard to imagine that if these clients have bought shares on the grounds that a company will make pre-tax profits of £50 million and it turns in only £40 million then questions will be asked. The buck is quickly passed and tends to stop with the company. There are few things to match the fury of a stockbroker who got his forecasts wrong. It is the kind of fury which a company does well to avoid and once again it is the finance director's responsibility to make sure that the figures match those anticipated by the City.

This relationship between companies and the City puts an entirely different perspective on the purpose of financial statements. They were originally intended to reflect how the entrepreneurs of the industrial revolution had looked after the cash, which had been put up at risk capital by shareholders to finance specific ventures. Today, though, the risk element of an investment, particularly in well-established business, is not linked to the company's operations but to the company's ability to keep the stock market sweet. Financial results have become a relative measure, not an absolute measure of success. Switching and swapping are the order of the day and a long term investment is one which won't be sold until a week on Tuesday.

The successful company is one which can strike the balance between giving out optimistic noises when the analysts' forecasts are being made and matching these later with the actual reported results. If a company is too conservative at the outset there will be no incentive for analysts to advocate that the shares be bought. But if it is too enthusiastic and the results do not match expectations, then not only will gains in the share price be lost but a lot of bad will is created. The whole aim is to create an atmosphere of 'buy the shares now and buy even more shares later'. The accomplished creative accountant, using the tools of his trade, will allow the company every opportunity to strike that balance, linking the absolute reality of trading performance with the relative illusions of reported results.

There is a danger, though, that this desire to keep the City happy and reap the rewards on an ever rising share price could get out of hand. For although the City is used as a collective noun to suggest a faceless legion of stockbrokers, bankers and financial institutions, it is in reality much more limited in its application. The City is rapidly becoming a handful of key analysts and institutions who between them have enormous power, and whose influence can make or break a company. The 'Big Bang' has radically changed the way the City is structured and operates, and the mighty financial conglomerates threaten to make a mockery of the concept of perfect knowledge. The perfect knowledge will be there all right, but in the hands of a few select organisations. Companies run the risk of becoming locked into a handful of these giants to the exclusion of the rest of the investment community.

That is a factor to be wary of in the future and for the time being many companies are more concerned with puffing up their share price. The creative accountant is supported in this task by a battery of press relations people, corporate communications consultants and investor relations advisers. Their life's work is to boost the company's share price and stock market rating. This may appear to be a worthy objective. A high share price, after all, reduces the chances of somebody else taking over a company, while at the same time increasing the chances of it making an acquisition of its own. Yet blind pursuit of a higher share price has its pitfalls.

Creative accounting, for all its scope to manipulate figures, cannot support the results of a company which is facing genuine and continuing trading difficulties. All that it can do is to defer and mitigate the bad news until there is a revival in trading fortunes. It cannot make bad news look good in perpetuity without resorting to out-and-out fraud. Therefore, if a company's share price tries to cross a bridge too far and comes unstuck, then untold damage can be done as a result of that setback. The wisest companies are those which use creative accounting to keep control not just of their figures but also of the share price itself. There is one well-known British company, a constituent of the FT 30 index, which does just this. The finance director has what he calls his bottom drawer, in which he keeps the fruits of his creative accounting — be they profits or losses — which he feeds out in order to ensure that the share price is kept within closely defined bands which reflect the company's genuine worth at a given moment in time.

When the creative accounting is so carefully controlled it is a relatively harmless weapon. It is merely reflecting the underlying trends in the value of the business, which would not always be apparent if the accounts were prepared and presented in accordance with a strict interpretation of the appropriate accounting rules and regulations. However, in the hands of a less scrupulous management it can be a highly dangerous instrument of deception. The investing community at large can be misled into making decisions on information which is neither full nor fair. Banks and other financiers might extend credit which, if the figures had been prepared in a different way, would have been withdrawn. Suppliers and other creditors may enter into a business relationship which otherwise would have been considered too risky.

The fact is, creative accounting is not just the prerogative of the quoted companies. Private companies have as much, if not more, to gain from manipulation of their annual accounts. This is particularly true of those which are considering making the transition either to the full Stock Exchange list or to the junior Unlisted Securities Market (perhaps better known as the Unlimited Surprises Market).

In these cases it is important to have created the right kind of trading record which will ensure that the flotation is accomplished with minimum fuss. Not only does the flotation provide the company with access to the massive funds of the existing City institutions but also presents the chance to entice the private investor to part with his hard-earned cash on the back of a campaign to promote wider share ownership.

That campaign had a tremendous boost from the give-away privatisation of British Telecom, which has perhaps created some illusions among the wider share owner. The double-your-money characteristic of the Telecom flotation was unique to that company. It was a never-to-be-repeated offer, well, not before the next big privatisation anyway. However, it has perhaps given the impression that playing the stock market is like stealing candy from a baby. Nothing could be further from the truth. Yet there are now large numbers of private investors eager to repeat their Telecom success, who have very little idea of the real rules of the stock market game they are playing. It is this ever growing group of shareholders who have the most to lose from irresponsible creative accounting.

There is no reason why they should be conversant with the techniques which are employed to massage the accounts. Indeed there is no reason why they should have any grounding in basic accountancy anyway. It is dividends and capital growth which are important. The annual report and accounts do not even merit a placing in many shareholders list of priorities. Yet this is the best opportunity the investor has to assess how his money is being managed. Ironically, the attitude among companies tends to be that, rather than to provide fuller and clearer statutory accounts, they concentrate instead on glossy superficial reviews of the business. It is a dangerous trend which will lead to a complete devaluation of the statutory accounts. The less attention paid to them, the more chance the creative accountant has of taking another step closer to the thin borderline which separates creativity from fraud. Once that divide is broken, then inevitably it will be the private share-holders who lose out most. There seems to be an unwritten rule that the big institutions will always suffer less then the small investor, be it as a consequence of fraud or simply of poor trading. This was illustrated by the tyre giant Dunlop's recent demise, which led to it being taken over by BTR — the indus-trial holdings group. The downturn in trading fortunes which left Dunlop on the verge of collapse was shared mainly by private investors. Most of the big institutions had sold out months earlier, confirming the view that perfect market information is only available to certain sections of the investing community. It leaves the small shareholders cruelly exposed to the wiles of the unscrupulous creative accountant. Not only are they last in line for being given the crucial information which might allow them to cut their losses and run, but more importantly they are actively dissuaded from taking an interest in the all-important financial statements which might give them a faint chance of seeing which way the wind is blowing.

But the use of creative accounting is not restricted to luring new investors into the company or keeping existing shareholders happy. It has also become very popular as a means of fighting takeover battles. The merger mania which has swept the country recently has forced both predators and defenders to search for new weapons which can be brought to bear on the opposition. Hardly a contested bid goes by without either or both sides resorting to creative accounting to bolster their own position, while at the same time criticising their opponent's methods of preparing and presenting financial information.

Yet this open acknowledgement of the distortion which takes place in financial statements seems to encourage the habit rather than pose questions about its acceptability. It is perhaps one of the few occasions when two wrongs seem to make a right, but then that is the creative accountant's stock in trade.

As long as there are contested bid battles to be fought then creative accounting will always have its part to play.

However, while large elements of the creative accountant's armoury are being openly put on display, it has to be said there has been a steady increase in the number of schemes which are not visible even to the most highly trained eye. This is the most sinister aspect of creative accountancy and stems from what has been called off balance sheet financing. This involves adapting schemes which, rather than manipulate existing figures, actually exclude them altogether from the financial statements. It is impossible to detect them even from a detailed analysis of the small print in the notes to the accounts. The reason for a company to take advantage of these schemes is normally to allow it to obtain funding which it would otherwise have been unable to secure. Debt levels may already be uncomfortably high, making it impossible for a company to secure the additional cash it needs to finance its capital investment programme. The answer to this rather embarrassing problem has come in the shape of a variety of off balance sheet financing schemes which have been devised and are now being actively marketed. These schemes threaten to undermine completely the dwindling credibility of the statutory accounts.

Whether the moves underway to try and improve the disclosure of such schemes will work remains to be seen. The problem for the accountancy profession is that it has condoned, and in some cases quite properly encouraged, an element of creative accounting, by its corporate clientèle. For it to turn round suddenly and say that off balance-sheet financing is the unacceptable face of creativity may leave it with some awkward questions to answer about the acceptibility of tactics and techniques which have been permitted in earlier accounting periods. The crucial question which has to be answered is, where should the line be drawn?

There is of course no answer. If there were, the line would have been drawn a long time ago and there would be no such thing as creative accounting. The reason why it has survived and thrived is that the system of accounting standards is itself designed to encourage an element of flexibility. The standards are not intended, despite their name, to lay down specific accounting treatments, but rather to narrow down the range of options which should be consistently applied in order to improve the comparability of accounts year on year and between one company and another. The system recognises that different businesses will find different methods of accounting more appropriate for reflecting their performance more fairly. But in trying to strike the balance between flexibility and fairness it has erred, and quite rightly according to most finance directors, on the side of flexibility. Unfortunately, this leaves a system which gives the impression of laying down uniform standards but in practice it merely endorses the differing accounting treatments which are available.

The upshot is that accounts can be prepared in accordance with accounting standards and still show entirely different results for the same set of transactions. There is no need for a company to resort to non-compliance with those standards in order to implement a particular creative accounting technique, in fact to do so would only attract unwanted attention. All that is required of company accounts is that they show a true and fair view, and nobody has ever managed to define quite what this means. With such vague terms of reference to which to work, the creative accountant's job is made that much easier and the auditor's job that much harder.

Although the auditor is employed in theory to protect and act on behalf of the shareholders, there is little effective opposition he can mount against the determined manipulator of figures. Many of the arguments for or against a particular accounting treatment are fought purely on subjective grounds. The questions are those of judgement not of fact: all the auditor has to rely on for his defence is the rather feeble support of the true and fair view. His job is made even harder by his own admission that the figures shown in the accounts could be wrong by between 5 and 10 per cent, perhaps even more, without any impairment of their truth and fairness. In the light of this it becomes very difficult to argue that a certain approach is definitely wrong, when no one has laid down what is definitely right. In the end the auditor has to settle for an element of bartering over specific treatments; he gets his way on some and allows the company to take a more liberal interpretation of the rules on others.

But it is not just the theoretical difficulties of technical interpretation which makes the auditor's job difficult. He also has to face some quite difficult practical and commercial pressures. These are imposed by the intense competitition in a stagnant audit market place. The companies are well aware of this and it is easy to see how an unscrupulous management might take advantage of this by subtly suggesting that failure to come round to their way of thinking on a particular issue might result, not directly of course, in the audit assignment being put out to tender. No firm likes to lose a client and it is surprising the extremes to which auditors will go in order to maintain cordial relations. This is not to suggest that the auditing profession is failing in its duties, but merely pointing out that when the question in dispute is one of judgement and there is no clearly defined right or wrong way of answering it, then pragmatism might prove to be the deciding factor.

It is not a situation which is likely to get any better. The competition in the market place is becoming increasingly intense, and some firms almost regard audit assignments as loss leaders which will give them the platform from which to sell their more lucrative services such as tax and management consultancy. And as the accounting practices, particularly the large international firms, set their sights on the type of corporate finance work which has traditionally been carried out by merchant banks, then the pragmatism might even be replaced by active incitement to adopt creative accounting techniques. There are already signs that this is happening, and these may still prove to be just the tip of the iceberg.

It is not, however, in the private sector alone where creative accounting is encountered: the public sector too has its own methods of manipulation. In these situations it is not the shareholders who are at risk but the taxpayers. The problem, though, is accentuated by the fact that the taxpayer has even less interest in the finances of the public sector than the small shareholder does in the accounts of his own company. The public's interest in the nationalised industries runs to such things as why trains don't run on time, why letters get lost in the post and why it takes the gasman such a long time to come and look at the boiler. Such practical questions are important, but they become even more so if they are asked against the background of a fuller understanding of a particular state industry's finances. At the moment the public is, by and large, quite happy to sit back and accept as gospel the figures which are broadcast as profits and losses for the year. The taxpayer seems quite happy to accept that the steel and coal industries lose lots of money while the gas and electricity industries make lots of money. No questions are asked about the methods of accounting which have been used to arrive at these conclusions.

Take the electricity industry for example. In 1983/84 it reported profits before interest of £914.4 million. It is a lot of money but not so much that the public gets too upset about it. However, that figure which is relayed to the taxpayer is based on current cost accounting principles which make an allowance for the impact of inflation. Had the electricity industry used the historical cost principles which are used in the private sector, the story would have been completely different. On the historical cost basis the pre-interest profits would have been £1,852.8 million. That is more than double the figure which is reported as the actual result for 1983/84. Suddenly questions might be asked about the prices which this public service company is charging to its customers, the taxpayer. The difference in the two figures works out at around a £20 a year reduction per person in electricity bills. On that basis some households would have been entitled to rebates. Yet the difference in the figures is purely a function of accounting treatment. It is exactly the same power stations producing exactly the same electricity for exactly the same consumers but one basis produces profits half those produced by another basis. And 1983/84 is not an isolated example. In 1984/85, when the results were affected by the miners' strike, the Electricity Council reported losses of £1,277.1 million before interest, using its favoured current cost accounting. Had it applied historical cost principles those losses would have reduced to just £146.6 million.

Clearly the chosen method of accounting will influence the budgets and forecasts which are critical in determining the level of price increases to be introduced. While the electricity industry insists on using current cost accounting which produce lower reported profits it will be able to justify more easily its price rises. Whether it is right to rely on the expediency provided by a particular accounting concept, which ironically, has now been totally discredited by the private sector and the accountancy profession is another matter altogether, but one which is very rarely discussed in the tap room or snug bar.

The use of creative accounting in determining pricing policies cannot, therefore, be underestimated. The Thames Water Authority showed this quite lucidly when it was attempting to resist government pressure for it to increase water rates. The government assumptions were based on current cost principles and showed that a price increase was needed in order for Thames to meet its required return on capital. The Thames assumptions, using historical principles, demonstrated quite the opposite and showed that more than adequate returns could be achieved without a price rise. Somebody had to be wrong.

It is not just in the area of pricing, however, where the chosen accounting treatment can influence the decision-making process. This was made horrifically clear during the bitter days of the year-long coal dispute. It was a conflict over pit closures. The National Coal Board insisted that it had to close uneconomic pits, while the union argued that the jobs could and should be preserved. However, one of the least controversial aspects of that dispute was over the definition of uneconomic. It was at the heart of the conflict yet it attracted very little publicity, and there is still no certainty that a satisfactory answer has been provided. The issue was raised by a team of independent accountancy academics who challenged the viability of certain key NCB accounting documents as the basis for making pit closure decisions. They raised important questions about fixed cost and overhead allocations which, if treated in different ways, produced different conclusions. It is a sad fact that people's jobs, and this is not just in the coal industry, could be put at risk simply because the accountants decide to treat certain costs in a particular way. Such arbitrary judgements are all well and good when the question is one of whether interest payments should be capitalised or not, but when that question could lead to somebody being deprived of their livelihood then a lot more care and caution is required from the creative accountant.

As the chapters unfold it will become clear that there is a tremendous amount of scope for making such arbitrary judgements. Carefully used the techniques outlined can provide a useful bridge between the artificial constraints of an annual reporting cycle and the reality of a trading cycle which may be either longer or shorter. Similarly, creative accounting can be used to iron out short term difficulties which might otherwise attract undue concern. However, the key to effective use of the various schemes is moderation. In the long run creative accounting is no substitute for sound trading and business development. Any attempt to make that substitution over a sustained period of time will result ultimately in catastrophe. It is, therefore, up to the company's management to use creative accounting with the integrity and respect which it deserves and it is up to individual shareholders to study financial statements more closely, to ensure that these standards are being upheld and maintained.

2

HOW to INCREASE INCOME

*I*ncome, for most individuals, is the cash they receive. Income for companies is anything but the cash they receive.

Once this deceptively straightforward view of the relationship between cash and income has been despatched swiftly out of the window, a company is then free to tinker with its reported figures almost at will. In the accounts the gross income may be described as sales or turnover or revenue. Such terms defy definition and the only thing that is certain is that they do not mean cash received.

The key to creative accounting in this section of the profit and loss account is the rather innocuous expression 'income recognition'. It may not sound particularly sinister but in essence it is an open invitation for a business to think of a number — any number — and disclose that as the company's turnover. The scope for turnover tampering will be determined, and often limited, by the nature of the company's activities. It is harder for a supermarket, which is predominantly a cash business, to manipulate its reported sales than it is for a computer leasing company, where the relationship between cash received and actual sale is more tenuous.

Within these practical constraints it is still possible for most companies to retain a substantial element of control over the figure which they report in their accounts as turnover. While income recognition is the practical key to creativity, the justification for the practice comes from the fact that companies are forced to report their results by reference to a financial year which, in most cases, is an entirely inappropriate period. There can be few companies which would say that a twelve month period was the best timescale over which to judge their business performance. A company which manufactures and sells baked beans might argue that a six-week financial period was the most appropriate. A construction company could argue that its financial period should last five years.

Tax and accounting laws overlook the practical problems which a business faces, and the annual reporting requirement has become an accepted if not always appropriate fact of life. However, this throws the door marked 'Creativity' wide open. Using the arguments of smoothing, and the ancient accounting principle of matching costs with income, a company is well placed to justify a wide and often ingenious array of methods to arrive at the figure which is reported as turnover.

Income recognition, like any good joke, depends for its success on timing. It is usually a question of deciding when and how much of any sales transaction will be included as part of the year's turnover. However, it can also involve some intricate mathematical gymnastics. The creative opportunities arising from income recognition are illustrated quite clearly by examining how Plessey, the electronics giant, accounts for sales of its System X digital telephone exchange equipment to British Telecom. Payment is made for the equipment in five separate stages: on order, on shipment, on installation, on commissioning and on completion of a warranty period which normally lasts twelve months. Plessey is careful not to divulge what proportion of the total price is handed over at each stage. That old favourite 'commercial confidentiality' prevents such disclosure it seems, even though the excuse would be more at home in a second-rate spy movie. However, even without knowing exactly when payments are made, it is still easy to see that Plessey is never able to forget that it has a choice.

It would be possible to present perfectly sound and logical reasons why the income could be recognised at any one of the five stages mentioned above. The picture is further complicated by the fact that the income does not have to be recognised and reported as sales on an all-or-nothing basis. It would be possible to account for the income on a phased basis. In Plessey's case, the company takes the full profit when the title passes to British Telecom, less a provision for the warranty. However, the System X transaction shows the kind of scope that is available to most other companies should they wish to play around with the amount actually reported as sales and the figure which will thus ultimately play an important part in determining what the profits for the year will be. Care is needed, however, since the chosen basis should be consistent one year with the next.

The impact which the timing of income recognition can have on a profit and loss account is quite considerable. Imagine two companies making exactly the same product and selling them to the same customer. Such a scenario is not far fetched since this is exactly the situation which prevails on System X, where GEC also supplies exactly the same exchange equipment again to British Telecom. Company A accounts for its sales on receipt of an order. Company B accounts for its sales 50 per cent on installation and 50 per cent on completion of the warranty period. Each company receives 12 orders, one a month for two years, each worth £1 million; it takes six months from the time of the order being received for the equipment to be installed and the warranty period is six months. Company A makes no provision on warranties even though the full price must be refunded if there is a problem. Half the equipment delivered will suffer from a problem within the warranty period.

It should be pointed out that both companies may choose to show the warranty payments as an expense rather than as a deduction from sales, but for the purposes of illustration it is assumed that the latter approach is adopted. From the example it is clear to see that in the three-year period both companies have done exactly the same amount of business. The net sales, after the deduction of the sales which were lost under the warranty arrangements, were £12 million. However, the way in which that figure is distributed over the three accounting periods varies quite dramatically. Company A would appear to

	Year 1 £m	Year 2 £m	Year 3 £m
Company A:			
Sales	12	12	—
less warranties	—	(6)	(6)
net	12	6	(6)
Company B:			
Sales	3	9	6
less warranties	—	(4.5)	(1.5)
net	3	4.5	4.5

be doing much better than its rival Company B with sales four times greater in year 1. It is still ahead in year 2 but then suddenly in year 3 Company A finds itself with negative sales of £6 million when Company B is reporting a same again £4.5 million.

The method which each company chooses will depend very much on its own particular needs. Company A, it seems, is suffering from short term deficiencies of income, and therefore needs to bring forward its sales as quickly as possible. Perhaps the management want to impress the stock market or they may be aware of some other contract work which will be coming on stream in year 3 and which would allow the company to maintain its sales performance. Company B, however, is more concerned with a steady flow of sales through the profit and loss account. The management is more concerned with consistency, and is keen to avoid any short term and sharp fluctuations in its reported figures. By adopting a more prudent approach Company B also has something in reserve should the going get tougher at a later date.

The question of putting income in your pocket and saving it for a rainy day is not restricted to the world of fairy tales, although it is easy to see why some observers believe that most sets of accounts owe more to Hans Christian Andersen than to financial reality. The concept of the bottom drawer is familiar to most finance directors: it is here they store those little bits of financial wizardry which can put a little more of a gleam on figures which would otherwise be lacking in lustre.

Company B, for instance, would be in a position, should it so wish, to conjure up additional sales in year 2 simply by changing its accounting policy to come into line with that of Company A. Assuming that the auditors could be convinced to go along with the scheme, it might even be possible for Company B actually to increase its reported sales to £21 million which, after deducting the increased warranty charge, would bring net sales for that year of £15 million. It is quite an increase.

Changing the accounting policy is a recurring theme in the world of creative accounting and one which auditors by and large are powerless to combat. Although consistency in presentation of figures is something for which companies are supposed to strive and something which auditors are supposed to encourage, the concept somehow manages to take on the characteristics of a Holy Grail which can never quite be tracked down. The clever finance director will be able to revolve the changes in accounting policies so that it is never immediately apparent to users of accounts exactly what is going on.

Not only is the lack of consistency a problem, but so too is the lack of comparability between companies which operate in similar industries. The way in which such quoted companies are valued on the stock market is by reference to the price earnings ratio. This is a simple discounting method used by analysts, whereby the share price is divided by the prospective earnings per share. The ratio in isolation is meaningless but it comes into its own when it is compared with the ratio of other companies in the same sector. In general, the higher the ratio, the greater the stock market's expectations about the company's future earnings, and therefore the greater its confidence in the business.

This is all well and good but there is a fundamental flaw in this key stock market analysis ratio when the earnings from different companies in the same sector are calculated in different ways. The price earnings ratio becomes totally discredited since it is no longer comparing like with like.

The computer leasing industry is a case in point. It sprang up in a small but quite significant way to take advantage first of the great tax advantages that the law permitted in the late seventies and second in response to a need for companies to have a flexible means of financing a heavy investment in computer technology. The computer leasing industry was new and sufficiently small to allow it to carve out its own ways of calculating its income and reporting its results. Unfortunately this mini industry didn't quite get around to sorting out common accounting standards with the result that income is reported in differing ways.

Most of the companies decided to enter the Nadia Komonech school of accounting thought with an accounting practice which defies gravity. In essence the computer leasing firms were writing business which, under traditional accounting practices, would result in a loss being disclosed. This, of course, is simply not on for a new company in a new industry. Profits were the order of the day and profits they were going to report. The way in which these profits were achieved was purely because of 'income recognition'.

The companies leased out computers which at the end of the lease they would still own and which they would then be able to sell. The view taken by the majority of those in the industry was that these 'residual values' could be recognised, in part, as income for the year in which the lease was first written. What this means is that the companies were taking as income, and thus profit, an item which would not be realised for some years, on the basis of the management's guess of what the computers could be sold for at that time. This may seem strange but it becomes even stranger when you consider that the values relate to computers which are subject to rapid technological change and very much in the hands of the vagaries of the market. However, the practice was accepted as being appropriate, and is now written into the computer leasing industry folklore.

One small problem arises, however, for not all the companies adopted the same approach. Dataserv does not take any account of residual values until they are actually realised. What price comparability?

The answer would appear to be perhaps, not very high. The stock market ratings afforded to the companies in the computer leasing sector seem to owe very little to the accounting policies of the individual businesses. The assumption must be that the market knows what it is doing but you cannot help but think that sometimes it is being swept away on the crest of a wave about which it knows or cares not a lot.

The market men may disagree, but there is one classic example of how the City can get well and truly caught out through its failure to appreciate the consequences of a particular accounting policy. This cautionary tale comes courtesy of a company called Micro Focus. No prizes for guessing that it is what is loosely known as a high-tech business. In essence the company sold its own software to other businesses with particular emphasis on the USA. The sales contracts, because of their nature, would only be realised in full over a period of time. The Micro Focus policy was to recognise the full sales value of the contract once it was firmly secured, even though in some cases payments from clients would fall due over several years.

This was all well and good in the company's formative years when the business was developing; the amounts involved on each contract were quite small and everything in the US computer industry garden was rosy. But as time flies, so times change, and this optimistic accounting policy suddenly began to look not just imprudent but dangerous. Diving into a swimming pool from a height of 300 feet is one thing, but diving in from the same height when there is no water in the pool is quite another.

The auditors called for a more realistic approach to sales recognition. After discussions which were no doubt free and frank, the company agreed to a change in accounting policy. Unfortunately for the stock market, it was not privy to these discussions and was therefore blissfully ignorant of the impact that the change would have on the Micro Focus results. The City had seen the company as something of a high flier and analysts were expecting pre-tax profits in the order of £5 million for the year — another healthy advance. The change in the accounting policy had the effect of deferring a large element of the company's sales, reflecting the more prudent approach, which sent reported profits tumbling. Instead of the £5 million which had been anticipated, Micro Focus reported a fall in profits to less than £1 million.

The stock market was horrified! The share price fell in the way that one does in a bad dream — seemingly endlessly — giving onlookers a taste of what Wall Street must have been like around 1929. The shares stood at 740p ahead of the results announcement. Within minutes the price was plummeting relentlessly downwards stopping 440p later at 300p. It may have looked like a reasonable reaction to a company which had quite clearly failed to live up to expectations. However, what must be remembered is that the sales figure was arrived at purely as the result of an acccounting adjustment. The underlying business was exactly the same, the number of contracts entered into was exactly the same; all that had changed was the accounting policy. Yet on the basis of an alteration which was done with the flick of a calculator the company's value was more than halved. Such is the power of creative accounting.

The Micro Focus tale is cautionary in nature. However, it did not appear to result in a flurry of changes as companies across the nation switched to more prudent accounting policies. Old habits die hard, and even harder when the result could be a reduction in profits.

It would be wrong, though, to assume that the most creative accounting is reserved only for the high technology sector. Certainly there is a lot of scope in this field because of its tender years. Without the benefit of hindsight it is hard for auditors to assess, with any degree of certainty, the realism of the assumptions which are presented in defence of an accounting policy. However, this does not preclude the more mature sectors from their own version of subtle manipulation. The construction industry, for instance, has a certain reputation for being somewhat selective in the way in which income is calculated. Again it is income recognition which provides the framework for the creativity, allowing the companies flexibility to take any amount of profit on construction work in progress.

As mentioned earlier some businesses find it harder than others to toy around with turnover. In any cash business, such as a supermarket, it is pretty difficult to massage the reported sales figure without resorting to downright fraud. However, with these few exceptions, the large majority of companies are allowed a tremendous amount of flexibility when calculating their income. As long as certain ground rules are adhered to and nothing too outrageous is countenanced, then the message seems to be 'take what you like when you like'.

Wouldn't life be much easier if individuals could employ the same tactics as those used by companies? The bowing and scraping which is needed to secure that extra few thousand on the mortgage could be forgotten once and for all. By bringing forward your salary from future years you could double your income at a stroke and no one would be any the wiser until of course you could no longer afford to make the repayments. Therein lies the restraining force on income creativity.

While it may be easy for companies to get away with rather strange accounting policies while all is going well, it becomes that much harder when the going gets a little rough. The hallmark of creative accounting is that it does not involve fraud. Fictitious sales are not conjured up out of thin air; it is the genuine sales which are just interpreted in slightly unusual ways. So when a company is consistently finding it hard to make any actual sales then creative accounting is of little assistance. All it can do is help smoothe over the rough patches or perhaps make the rate of decline appear a little slower than it is in reality. Arguments may be found to defend the former but not the latter.

Whatever the moral rights and wrongs of income manipulation, there is no doubt that it is a valuable and much used tool for most companies. While it is permitted under company law and accounting rules it will continue unabated. All that shareholders and other users of accounts can do is to be on their guard, scrutinise the accounting policy on turnover more closely and read the financial statements with more than a modicum of scepticism.

3

HOW to EXPAND EXPENSES

*I*t is impossible to examine the creative accounting techniques used to manipulate a company's costs and expenses as disclosed in the profit and loss account in isolation from the corresponding balance sheet items. Unlike income, where the company has some choice over when it will be recognised, that luxury is not generally afforded to expenses. The general rules of prudence dictate that they must be accounted for as they are incurred or anticipated. Therefore a company must look to the balance sheet for help, relying mainly on the subjective assessment which is necessary in determining the extent of liabilities and provisions to bring it some flexibility on the amounts which are charged to the profit and loss account. Alternatively, it may try and reduce its expenses either by treating them as capital or deferring them to a later period through a balance sheet carry forward.

Most of the techniques and their effects are described in more detail in the specific chapters dealing with the balance sheet items, but it is useful to provide a brief summary which gives a taste of the range of options which are available.

The most effective way of deferring costs to a later period is to carry them forward to the next accounting period as part of the company's closing stock. This is possible because the relevant rules and regulations allow the attributable costs and overheads relating to the production process to be included in the year end stock valuation.

The effect of this is to take some of the costs out of charge in one year and push them forward into the next. By a judicious allocation of these costs and particularly overheads the company can artificially boost the value of its stock and thereby reduce the cost of sales for the year and increase reported profits. However, this is only a deferral and while the cost of sales is reduced in the first year it will of course be increased in the second, and the company has to be careful that it does not put too much pressure on its year end stock valuation of that subsequent period.

If the company wants to exclude costs completely rather than merely defer them it has to look to the possibility of capitalising the expenses. The rules on what can be justifiably treated as capital rather than revenue expenditure owe more to tax than accounting rules, but there are still some clear opportunities for cost deferment and exclusion. The first stems from the option which companies have to capitalise the interest on borrowings which are used to finance the construction and development of fixed assets. Rather than being charged to profit and loss, the interest is added to the cost of the asset. In most cases this will eventually have to be charged to the profit and loss account by way of the depreciation charge. However, that charge will be spread over the life of the asset which could be quite long. In some cases it is possible for the interest charge to be avoided altogether. This is where it relates to the cost of acquiring land which is not generally subject to depreciation. The capitalised interest is therefore perpetually carried forward as part of the company's fixed assets.

A variation on this theme is available through the capitalisation of research and development costs. The principle is the same as for interest charges, and again these costs might ultimately find their way into the profit and loss account by way of a depreciation charge. This approach is particularly appropriate for companies which find themselves incurring high computer software costs and allows them to spread the charge more evenly over a longer period of time.

A further method of effectively excluding costs is to disclose certain items below the line as extraordinary items.

Although the costs are quite clearly reported they are actually excluded from the company's pre-tax profits record and, more importantly, from its earnings per share record. This is because extraordinary items are deemed to distort the company's true trading record and are therefore discounted. This is particularly important for earnings which are a key component in the price earnings ratio which is used by the stock market as its most important performance indicator. By taking advantage of the rather vague rules defining when an item is extraordinary and disclosed below the line or exceptional and thus taken above as part of pre-tax profits for the year, a company can boost its earnings quite substantially.

The impact of the extraordinary items ruse is to disclose the charges and costs which have been incurred but in effect take them direct to reserves since they are disclosed below the line. This is a tactic which is by and large frowned upon by the accountancy profession although there are specific opportunities for doing just this.

One such opportunity comes from the treatment of goodwill. Many companies now use artificial financing arrangements to avoid creating goodwill in the first place, thus relieving them of the requirement to write it off. Two methods of achieving this write-off are allowed. The company can either amortise the intangible asset through an annual charge to the profit and loss account or write the entire amount off at a stroke direct to reserves. Clearly the former approach will serve to depress reported profits, so many companies are avoiding the charge by adopting the immediate write-off method.

Reserve accounting can also be used to deal with exchange losses which arise on the translation of long term borrowings denominated in foreign currencies. Normally these losses, and any gains, would be reported as part of the trading result for the year. However, if the company can demonstrate that the overseas loan was taken out either to finance or provide a hedge against a foreign equity investment, then any exchange losses can be offset against the gains on the translation of the relevant equity investment. The net gain is then taken direct reserves, thus keeping the unfortunate exchange loss well away from the reported profits for the year.

Apart from these notable exceptions there are few other opportunities for a company to take costs direct to reserves. However, there is a subtle alternative which allows companies to account for certain charges through the balance sheet rather than profit and loss account and which is quite devastating when used alongside the extraordinary items technique.

Quite simply, a company which recognises that it will be forced to incur substantial costs over a period of time, perhaps relating to a major rationalisation or restructuring programme, makes a provision for all the anticipated expenses at one fell swoop. The size of the provision and the general nature of the costs should ensure that the company is able to disclose the charge below the line as an extraordinary item even though large elements of the expenditure may not fall into this category. Thus the company excludes the entire charge from the earnings and pre-tax profits calculations. As part of the accounting process the company sets up a provision for the rationalisation programme costs which is then carried forward in the balance sheet. As the costs of the programme are incurred they are charged against the provision and thus excluded from the profit and loss account.

Even if the provisions are not set up with the help of an extraordinary item, they are still an effective way of taking all the bad news in one year rather than spreading it across a period of time. This serves to give the impression that the company is on the road to recovery when in reality it is still in the process of knocking itself into some kind of shape.

Another approach to the problem is simply to ignore impending liabilities altogether. This is a less prudent approach but one which might be forced on the company as a result of a particular set of circumstances which have perhaps resulted in a poor trading performance which it does not want to be made any worse.

The general rule is that any such potential liability should be recognised as soon as it is discovered or anticipated. However, there will be situations where the company could argue that the likelihood of the liability crystallising is so remote that there is no need to make a provision. It is a rather desperate measure, however, and by and large should be resisted.

The same advice applies to the avoidance of other provisions. These may relate to the deferred tax charge, bad debts, warranty claims or some similar item. All require a charge to be made to the profit and loss account and failure to make the necessary provisions could result in more severe problems in the longer term. If possible, companies should set up excessively prudent provisions in the years when profits are strong thus presenting the option not to increase them when profits become weak. It all helps to avoid the unusual fluctuations in the profits performance which are most unwelcome in the City.

There are, of course, some provisions which have to be provided year in year out. The depreciation charge, for instance, is difficult to avoid. However, even here the company can retain some control over the level of the costs incurred simply by changing the rates at which it is charged on the relevant fixed assets. Depreciation can either be accelerated by shortening the estimated life of the fixed asset, or slowed down by extending the life.

There is also scope for playing around with residual values; these are the amounts which an asset would realise when sold. The residual values are not part of the depreciation equation and any change to them would constitute an error in original estimation. The financial effects of making a change would therefore be classified as prior year adjustments: any damage is thus limited to previous rather than current year profits. However, some companies treat any consequent over depreciation as a write back to profits in the year of the reassessment. For companies which want to depress their profits, perhaps transport companies wanting to push through fare increases, then they can charge the higher replacement cost depreciation charge over an asset's historical cost life.

Not all transport companies want to depress their profits particularly when they are just starting out in life. One way to improve their profits is not to provide for any overhead costs, but when maintenance of the vehicles, aircraft or vessels is required then the bulk of such costs is capitalised and then depreciated over time. When the company is bigger and more soundly based it can then provide for overhead expenditure in advance to assist in profits smoothing.

One final avoidable cost is the contribution the company makes to its employees' pension fund. Normally such an action would be greeted with howls of protest not just from the workforce but also from existing pensioners who would justifiably be concerned that their rights and benefits would be jeopardised. However, a variety of circumstances have contrived to allow many companies to take just this action without unduly ruffling any feathers. The legacy for this comes from the massive surpluses which have been run up by many pension schemes. Their swollen assets are well in excess of those needed to meet their future commitments. This has come about as a function of shrinking staff levels and a rampant stock market which has not just produced excellent capital growth but has also provided returns well ahead of the increase in rates of pay. The Inland Revenue is applying gentle pressure on companies to run down these surpluses and one of the most effective means of so doing is to reduce or abandon altogether the employer's contributions to the fund. This pensions holiday can be linked with improved benefits or an employees' holiday as well, although neither is a prerequisite for the company itself to take advantage of the reduction in its own costs.

All these creative accounting techniques are explained in greater detail elsewhere. However, one cost which is not touched upon is the dividend payments which a company makes to its shareholders. The opportunities for manipulating this figure are somewhat limited. Shareholders tend to get a bit angry if a company makes out it is paying 8p a share and in fact hands over only 2p.

However, the dividend should not be underestimated as an important weapon, not in the context of the hand to hand combat of the creative accounting arena but more in the theatre of psychological warfare. The dividend is clearly important for shareholders. It is one of the prime reasons for investing in a company in the first place and it is normally the most tangible contact which investors have with the company which they own. Certainly the value of the shares is also important, but paper profits are no compensation for the hard cash which the dividend provides. For this reason the distribution policy which a company adopts is an important tool in either maintaining or improving confidence in the business.

That policy is at its most effective and most dangerous during times of financial difficulties. A company can often deflect any undue criticism of poor trading results by maintaining its dividend payments. The capital value of the shares may deteriorate but as long as the dividends are being handed over this tends not to cause too much concern. The official explanation for this is that the maintained dividend is a clear indication of the management's confidence in the future prospects of the business. As the share price falls further so the rate of the dividend yield increases. However, these explanations and reasonings tend to mask the shareholders' underlying relief at getting their hands on the cash.

The company is able to pursue an aggressive and perhaps imprudent dividend policy because it is allowed to dip into its accumulated distributable reserves in order to make the payment. Persistent use of reserves for funding dividend payments should put shareholders on their guard. In fact the reverse tends to happen, and it is the companies which cut or withhold dividends which tend to suffer more from an adverse shareholder reaction. Hell hath no fury like an investor deprived of his divi it seems.

The chosen dividend policy can be a very useful indicator of the company's underlying performance. Excessive generosity or imprudence may be a sign that the company is desperate to maintain and boost confidence in it. On the other hand if the company appears to be overly imprudent and even a little on the mean side it may well suggest that it has some short term cash flow problems. A more regular analysis of the dividend cover is called for to ensure that the company's dividend policy is being consistently maintained and that it reflects the trading performance. Note also the increase in the number of companies offering more shares instead of cash by way of a dividend.

While the dividend payments may be useful as a psychological accounting tool, it is not one which can be used too frequently, and both management and shareholders alike should be well aware of the inherent dangers of excessive manipulation. The same is true of rights issues which are regarded by some as a means of getting the shareholder to pay for his own dividend.

4

HOW to PILFER the PENSION FUND

*T*he company pension fund is not the most obvious
target of the creative accountant's attention. The very
thought of tampering with the rights of widows and orphans
and long-suffering and serving employees is rather distasteful.
For a long time the reluctance to steal sweets from children
kept pension schemes safe from any creative accounting. This
safety was enhanced by the fact that the individual funds, plans
and schemes were actually independent of the companies themselves. They were controlled by trustees whose responsibilities
were to the pensioners and current contributing members, not
to the company.

However, in times of crisis no area of a company's operations is immune to the creative accounting epidemic, and
pension funds were forced to line up with all the other areas of
the balance sheet and profit and loss account for detailed
inspection. It soon became apparent that many pension schemes
were actually faring better than the companies themselves. It
was particularly true in the labour intensive manufacturing
companies. They had been badly hit by the recession.
Operations had been cut back, factories closed down and large
chunks of the workforce made redundant in the process. Mean-
while, the pension scheme with its assets invested in the
booming equity markets had gone from strength to strength.
In some cases the market capitalisation of the pension fund was
as much as that of the company itself. It was clear from the

31

actuary's report that the fund's assets were more than enough to meet the projected liabilities leaving huge surpluses which were no longer required. These surpluses were eyed jealously by finance directors who immediately set about devising ways of getting their hands on them. The task was, however, to prove to be easier to talk about in theory then to execute in practice.

First, though, it is useful to assess how these surpluses have arisen. It is largely a function of declining workforces, rates of return which outstrip wage inflation and a huge increase in the value of the funds' assets. The British Airways pension funds' report reveals that in the 1984 calendar year a rate of return of 18.6 per cent was achieved and this with an investment strategy which was admitted to be wrong because it had been underweight in UK ordinary shares and overweight in property. The median rate of return for comparable funds was 20 per cent compared with an increase in retail prices of 4.9 per cent and a rise in national average earnings of 6.6 per cent.

This is not just a single exceptional year. In the five years up to 1984 the annual return on self administered pension fund assets was 22.2 per cent for the private sector and 23.3 per cent for local government schemes. In the same period the annual growth in earnings averaged 10.3 per cent while prices rose by an average 8.4 per cent a year. This boom of the 1980s did little more than compensate fund managers for the lean years of the 1970s. Investment returns of private sector schemes averaged just 11.3 per cent between 1963 and 1984 compared with average earnings increases of 11.2 per cent and an annual average increase in prices of 9 per cent. More marked has been the rapid increase in the value of the assets under management. Estimates for 1985 suggest that at the end of that year the self-administered pension funds controlled assets worth around £150 billion compared with just £40 billion at the end of 1979. The combination of these factors over the last five years has brought a steady rise in surpluses within pension funds throughout the 1980s. One estimate suggested that these are worth around £50 billion in total, although that figure has been hotly disputed.

The true figure will probably never be revealed but be it £5 billion or £50 billion is rather immaterial. The fact is that there are big surpluses which companies can use to improve their own financial position. Ironically the impetus for action on the surplus came more from the Inland Revenue than from the corporate sector. The Revenue was conscious that the huge surpluses which had been run up were actually going untaxed, a legacy of the tax free status afforded to pension schemes. From its point of view this was not a satisfactory situation. The Revenue clearly wanted to get its hands on the tax and began putting covert pressure on companies and their pension funds to reduce the level of their surpluses. At first the action to remove those surpluses went largely unnoticed, but the question achieved some notoriety following the rather public and ultimately unsuccesful attempt by Gomme Holdings, the furniture company, to clawback its pension fund surplus.

The company discovered that it had a surplus of £4.1 million in the fund. It announced that it intended to wind up the old scheme and replace it with a new plan which would provide improved benefits and would also result in employees being given a holiday from making their own contributions. Gomme estimated that the cost of the new scheme would absorb £1.2 million of the surplus leaving £2.9 million which would be refunded to the company and which it could then use in its own business. This would have been a very welcome bonus for the company bringing it much needed liquid funds while at the same time providing the employees and existing pensioners with a better deal. Unfortunately for Gomme the Inland Revenue did not share this enthusiasm for the new arrangements and effectively vetoed the deal. It prompted the government to issue some broad guidelines on how companies should deal with surpluses.

In essence those guidelines suggested that where a surplus is not too large, then the Inland Revenue will normally accept that this is a short term fluctuation in the long term fortunes of the pension scheme and will therefore leave it unchallenged until the next actuarial valuation of the fund is due. If the surplus is unacceptably large then the Revenue will allow a company temporarily to reduce the level of the employer's contribution to the fund which should generally be sufficient to reduce the surplus to acceptable levels by the time of the next valuation. However, if that is insufficient then all that is required should be a reduction in the long term contribution rate. In cases where the surplus is so large that it threatens the exempt approved status of the scheme then improvements may be made to the scheme's benefits, although the Revenue will not insist on these being made in all cases. Similarly the contributions to the scheme can be completely suspended — a pensions holiday — by the employer and if necessary the employees. If a complete contributions holiday, perhaps for five years, still fails to produce the desired reduction of the surplus then the Revenue might then require part or all of it to be refunded to the company itself. Even so, these cases will be rare and if a surplus still remains after a five-year contributions holiday then there is no guarantee that a refund will be automatically granted. The key question is whether the surplus is so large that special measures need to be taken in order to deal with it. The company's own financial position is something of an irrelevancy until it is apparent that after a five-year contribution holiday the surplus will not be satisfactorily reduced. In such cases it will be appropriate to allow a refund but it may well be that a longer contributions holiday is a better remedy. The overall message is 'Reduce surpluses, but in a specified way, and don't expect to secure a refund as a matter of course.'

The effect of these guidelines from the government is not to deter but to encourage companies to take advantage of their pension fund surpluses. The clawback of surpluses is not ruled out altogether and Redfearn National Glass is just one company which succeeded in obtaining one under the new guidelines and there are others which have done the same. Certainly it is more difficult for a business to simply clawback surpluses either in cash or near cash form, but there are still a large number of creative accounting opportunities available.

If anything those opportunities are enhanced by not reclaiming the surplus and instead taking advantage of the contributions holiday which is advocated so firmly in the government's guidelines. This is because the cost of the company's contributions to its pension fund represent a charge to profit for the year and therefore, by manipulating that charge, the creative accountant has a golden opportunity to influence reported profits for the year. The scope is increased by the fact that there is not necessarily a direct link between the physical amount of cash which is handed over to the pension fund and the amount which is actually registered in the profit and loss account as the charge for the year.

This is yet another anomaly thrown up by the accruals concept of accounting which is cherished so dearly by the accountancy profession. Essentially this dictates that revenues and costs should be recognised as they are earned or incurred not as money is received or paid and then matched with one another insofar as their relationship can be established. The thrust of the concept is to spread the company's income and expenses more smoothly over a period of time, thus avoiding short term fluctuations which will perhaps distort the company's trading performance.

That concept is recognised in the accounting guidelines on how companies should deal with pension contribution costs. These tend to ignore the physical cash payments looking much more at the long term payments profile which reflects the long term nature of the pension fund. The suggestion is that a company should decide on the amount which should be charged in order to meet its responsibilities and liabilities to the fund and then stick with it. The same amount should be charged each year irrespective of the cash paid over to the fund. Amendments are only made to the annual charge to bring it more into line with the contributions level determined by actuarial valuations.

Unfortunately, these guidelines are far removed from the reality of the pension fund surplus situation and they have tended to be ignored by companies which have opted for pension contributions holidays as a means of bringing down surpluses. This was clearly demonstrated by Lucas Industries when it revealed to an unsuspecting stock market that it was the beneficiary of a surplus and was going to take a pensions holiday. The impact of that decision, it said, would be to increase its pre-tax profits by a massive £20 million in each of its next two financial years. The effect was quite dramatic as the share price leapt upwards in response to the news.

The Lucas contributions holiday has been one of the biggest both in terms of the amount of the saving and the reaction of the share price. But it is far from being the only company in this position. It is becoming a growing feature of company announcements that a pensions holiday has been taken, thus boosting reported profits and helping that all important earnings per share figure which has a large bearing on the stock market rating.

However, the approach that a company takes on its contributions will be determined very much by its own requirements. If a business is short of profits in a particular year then the charge to the profit and loss account can be abandoned completely. However, if profits are not a particular problem the company may simply decide to carry on making the charge even though no physical cash payments are being made. One way to do this is to take the charge above the line which impacts on pre-tax profits and those attributable to shareholders, but then to make an adjustment below the line which ensures that the company's reserves reflect the benefit of the holiday.

The company must also decide what level of disclosure it is prepared to make about its approach on pension contributions and indeed on the level of any surpluses in the scheme itself. The Lucas announcement was bound to improve its share price. By making the statement independently of any results announcement the increase in the share price was perhaps greater than it would have been if the news had been given to the stock market as an explanation for profits which were £20 million more than the City had been expecting. There may be situations, however, where a company is quite content with its stock market rating and therefore there is no need for such a boosting statement.

Instead the contributions holiday can be tucked away quietly within the profit and loss account. Indeed, if the holiday has actually helped a company to achieve levels of profit which would not otherwise have been reached, it may be better to maintain a cloak of silence. The last thing a company wants is for the shareholders to know the extent of the contribution to profits from the pensions holiday and then conclude that the underlying trading performance was quite poor.

Once again it becomes a question of horses for courses. The decision on whether or not to take a pensions holiday, and if so how to account for it and disclose it, will depend on the company's individual circumstances. The same is true of the attitude to disclosing information on a pension fund surplus. There is no legal requirement for a company to disclose in its own accounts, the level of any surplus. However, there may well be situations where it is prudent to do so. For instance, where a company feels it may be vulnerable to a takeover, it might decide that to let on about the hidden asset of a pension fund surplus would be an open invitation for a predator to step in. However, that same asset might also be used as an argument to suggest that the company is actually worth a lot more than its stock market price suggests. When BTR, the industrial holding company, took control of Dunlop, the ailing tyre giant, the bid battle which preceded the ultimate takeover ignored completely the massive pension fund surplus which had built up in Dunlop's pension fund. That surplus, about which very little is known even now, may well have been quite significant in the context of Dunlop's dilapidated net assets. Whether BTR was aware of this hidden asset is not clear, but the fact is that it obtained a highly valuable surplus for nothing.

As long as these surpluses are around, then there will be scope for companies to take advantage of them in their accounts as they gradually run them down. However, the sooner action is taken, the better. A collapse of the equity market would slash pension fund asset values at a stroke, which in turn would hit the level of the surplus. The smaller the surplus the less chance there is for effective accounting to be implemented.

A further limitation on the scope for taking advantage of the pension fund surplus lies in the clear moral issues which cannot be ignored when a company is deciding on a particular course of action. The fact that the company's approach will affect not just existing pensioners but also the current workers who make their regular contributions must temper any decision. If a company is seen to be running down the surplus for its own benefit rather than for the people who 'own' it, it may run into practical difficulties and also attract adverse publicity. It is therefore important for the company to ensure that it is even-handed in its choice of action.

Some improvement in benefits for existing pensioners will go some way to deflecting trouble, and consultation with the existing workforce will also make the implementation of any surplus reduction programme much easier to put in place. It does not look good when a company takes a contributions holiday for itself but insists that the employees carry on making their contributions, and in extreme cases it may result in labour relations problems with might otherwise have been avoided.

It is important then for the management to balance its loyalty to its shareholders with that of its loyalty to the employees. Judging from the success which Lucas has had in implementing its pension contributions simply by extensive consultation with employee representatives, the moral issues can be addressed equivocally and without jeopardising the reduction scheme itself. The nature and size of a pension fund surplus should ensure that both the company, the existing pensioners and the current employees can share in its reduction equally.

It will be the company which tries to be underhand and greedy which runs the risk of goading its workforce into industrial action which is both unnecessary and counter-productive. Do right by the lads and the lads will do right by you.

Assuming this practical and altogether necessary attention is given to the moral and social issues relating to pension fund surpluses then the creative accountant will be at liberty to carry out his work free of all liens and encumbrances. The benefits which subsequently accrue to the company as a consequence of this added, and in many cases bonus, flexibility will actually work to everyone's advantage since the impact on the profit and loss account will inevitably lead to a much smoother ride for the share price, which should provide the kind of stability which shareholders and workers alike will prefer.

5

HOW to PAMPER PRESENTATION

*T*he old man stared down wistfully at the sprawling concrete mass which masqueraded as a housing estate. The estate had a reputation for crime and violence. The old man looked up and in a quiet sad voice said: 'It's not the people, it's the way we package them.'

This sorry reflection of urban decay has a poignant message for the creative accountant. That same man might look at a set of accounts and say: 'It's not the figures, it's the way we package them.'

There is no doubt that one of the simplest ways of applying a coat of gloss to otherwise dull figures is to present them in the accounts more attractively. This does not mean filling the annual report with pictures of the chairman at the works disco and snaps of a junior trade minister shaking hands with the marketing director. Such superficial camouflage has its part to play but does little to disguise the true meaning of the financial figures as reported.

Successful creative presentation does not have its roots in design consultancy and artistic impression but in the flexibility which is offered by the accounting rules which govern the disclosure and treatment of certain key items and transactions. In practice, presentation can be improved by some careful and liberal interpretation of the rules on extraordinary items, associated companies, prior year adjustments and changes in accounting policy. All of these offer tremendous scope for

for presenting figures in a much better light.

By far the most popular method of improving the presentation of figures is to take advantage of the vague rules on when an item should be classified as extraordinary rather than exceptional. It may seem a rather academic distinction perhaps more appropriate for discussion at a use of English language seminar or by the Call My Bluff panelists. Not so. The distinction has a critical importance for the creative accountant. The reason stems from the way in which the key stock market price earnings ratio is calculated. In itself that calculation is quite simply the share price divided by earnings per share. However, the earnings figure excludes any impact of extraordinary items which are disclosed 'below the line', although below the belt would sometimes appear to be a more appropriate description.

The logic for excluding extraordinary items from the earnings attributable to shareholders is well-founded. It is reasonable that the profits reported by a company should only be those from its normal recurring activities and operations. Any one-off items deriving from unusual transactions or events should be kept separate. This fits in with the stock market's traditional analysis using the price earnings ratio. This key indicator assumes that past earnings are a reasonable guide to a company's future earnings power. It is therefore important to exclude these unusual items if a genuine earnings record is to be charted and the company's performance assessed. Similarly, since the price earnings ratio is a relative indicator when used to compare one company with another, it is important that such items are treated in a consistent fashion by all companies.

Unfortunately that logic presents little more than a wonderfully naïve series of principles which would be applied in the perfect world. But this is not a perfect world, and while most companies pay token lip-service to the ideals which underpin the accounting standard setters thinking, in practical terms they ignore them completely. And although the rules on when an item should be treated as extraordinary are clearly set out, the nature of their wording is such that it can be interpreted in numerous ways.

The most recent definition of an extraordinary item from the Accounting Standards Committee (ASC) is one which: 'derives from events or transactions that fall outside the ordinary activities of the company and which are both material and expected not to recur frequently or regularly. They do not include items which, though exceptional by virtue of size or incidence (and which therefore require separate disclosure), fall within the ordinary activities of the company. They do not include prior year items merely because they relate to a prior year.'

That is the official version but there does seem to be another method of deciding whether an item is extraordinary or exceptional which is used more regularly in practice by companies. This is known as 'the try it on the chairman and see what he says' method. It is perhaps not as sophisticated as that suggested by the accountancy profession but it does seem to find a lot of support in boardrooms up and down the country. There are several variations on the theme but basically the method works as follows.

The finance director discovers that one overseas division has made an uncharacteristic loss of £1 million. He goes to tell the chairman who says: 'How extraordinary! Let's hope it doesn't happen again.' The finance director leaves with a knowing look on his face. Minutes later he discovers that another overseas division has made an uncharacteristic profit of £1 million. Off he trots to tell the chairman who retorts: 'What an exceptional performance. Let's hope they keep it up.' Exit the finance director with another knowing look to keep him company.

Do not let this contemptuous appraisal of financial decision-making detract from the genuinely biased view that companies take of extraordinary items. The basic rule does seem to be that all big losses are extraordinary and go below the line while all big profits are exceptional and go above the line to boost earnings per share.

The effect of treating items as either extraordinary or exceptional can have a dramatic impact on the reported profits of a company and on its earnings per share. Blatant abuse of the rules may well be taken on board by the stock market in the year that the offence occurs and the share price discounted to reflect this. However, this tends to be a short term reaction; any drop in the share price may be later recovered and, of course, the artificially inflated earnings and profits figure then take their place in the company's performance record. Once in place the figures are there for keeps and how they were achieved will usually be overlooked when the company's performance over a period of time is analysed.

The impact on the results is shown in this simple example. Three companies, A, B and C operate in the same industry. Each makes trading profits of £30 million. Because of falling demand all three companies have to reorganise the business and sack a large number of workers, although the factory at which they worked continues to operate with reduced manning. The cost of reorganisation is £10 million. At the same time the companies each sell off a shareholding in an associated company which has been held for five years, at a profit of £5 million. No tax or dividends are payable. All three companies have 10 million ordinary shares in issue. Each company treats the items as illustrated on page 44.

It is clear from the example that the different treatments bring vastly different results. For instance Company A's profits and earnings per share are 75 per cent higher than those of Company C. Yet it is not inconceivable that all three companies could put forward arguments which suggest that their presentation is the correct one. It therefore leaves the stock market analysts with something of a problem. Each company is reporting exactly the same results and transactions, but by presenting them in a different way the price earnings ratios are completely at odds with each other. Assuming a stock market price for the shares of all three companies of 10p the price earnings ratio of Company A is a little under 3, Company B's is 4 and Company C is selling on 5 times historical earnings.

The conclusion that might reasonably be drawn, assuming that the average price earnings ratio for the sector is 4, is that Company A's shares are undervalued and should therefore be

	A	B	C
	£m	£m	£m
Trading profit	30	30	30
Exceptional item (sale of associate)	5	—	—
Exceptional items net (sale of associate and reorganisation costs)	—	(5)	—
Exceptional item (reorganisation costs	—	—	(10)
Profit attributable to shareholders	35	25	20
Extraordinary item (reorganisation costs)	(10)	—	—
Extraordinary item (sale of associate)	—	—	5
Transfer to Reserves	25	25	25
Earnings per share before extraordinary items	3.5p	2.5p	2.0p
Earnings per share after extraordinary items	2.5p	2.5p	2.5p

bought until the shares reach 14p, Company B's shares are fairly valued and should be held but Company C's shares are too expensive and should be sold until the shares fall to 8p. All three companies would then have price earnings ratios of 4.

This is of course an over-simplified assessment of the situation and assumes all kinds of things about the working of the stock market which would never apply in practice. However, the underlying thrust of the analysis is perfectly valid. It shows quite simply that by manipulating the way in which the figures are presented in the accounts the company can influence the valuation of its share price.

This situation has not been lost on the ASC which recognised that the original rules were not working as well as it was intended when it issued revised proposals for dealing with the subject. It took them 10 years to get round to that revision. The problem was spelt out quite clearly in the preface to the revised proposals which said: 'One of the objectives of accounting standards is to narrow the areas of difference and variety in accounting practice. There has been considerable inconsistency between companies in their classification of extraordinary and exceptional items. The ASC continues to believe that what is extraordinary in one business will not necessarily be extraordinary in another, but considers that greater consistency is desirable and to this end proposes additional guidance on extraordinary items.'

To say that 'greater consistency is desirable' is something of an understatement. It is a bit like saying 'world peace is desirable'. Honourable these objectives may be, but to make them work requires a tremendous amount of goodwill on the part of those who influence such things. Frankly, there is no incentive for a company to take the path marked good and righteous when everybody else is taking the sly and devious route and not suffering unduly. Those companies which do stick firmly by the rules are normally praised by the City analysts, who will outwardly congratulate them on being so brave and honest in taking the bad news above the line while inwardly shaking their heads and saying 'silly person'.

That inconsistency is shown quite clearly in the way that House of Fraser and Debenhams treated property sales. Both companies are in exactly the same line of business which is essentially running department stores. Some consistency might have been expected but in their accounts for 1985 the two companies reveal a starkly contrasting view on property disposals.

The House of Fraser accounting policy on property sales reads: 'Surpluses realised on the sale of properties and fixed asset investments, less the reorganisation and closure costs which precede and relate directly to the sale of properties . . . are reported as extraordinary items as these transactions are not considered to be part of the ordinary activities of the group.'

The Debenhams accounting policy on the disposal of properties says: 'Where the group disposes of substantially all its interest in a property, the profit or loss, being the difference between the net proceeds of sale and historical cost, is taken to profit and loss account and included in other items.'

The effect of the two different approaches to dealing with the same item was that in 1985 Debenhams boosted its above the line profits by £3.5 million as a result of its property disposals. House of Fraser disclosed a surplus of just under £1 million below the line as extraordinary income.

Sadly, the ASC's revision may be a case of too little too late. Its points of clarification tend to concentrate on the treatment of reorganisation, rationalisation and redundancy costs. These were a regular feature among manufacturing companies in the early part of the decade as they reeled under the crushing blows dealt by the devastating recession which hit the country. Factories were closed, workers were cast onto the ever lengthening dole queues and companies desperately tried to regroup in order to survive. The result was massive and unavoidable costs which had to be shown somewhere in the accounts. Many of these costs were clearly extraordinary and could justifiably be disclosed below the line. By the same token some were clearly not, but still managed to sneak below the line.

The standard practice seemed to be that whenever the three 'R's, reorganisation, rationalisation and redunancy were involved, then the costs were automatically treated as extraordinary items. The monotonous regularity with which these items appeared in company accounts, and the awesome size of the costs involved, tended to overshadow the way in which they were treated. It is only now that the three 'R's are less frequent visitors to financial statements that attention has focused more closely on the accounting treatment developed.

However, it would be wrong to suggest that the extraordinary/exceptional item dilemma has disappeared completely. Many company auditors still find this the most contentious presentation issue with which they have to deal. The magnitude may have fallen, but the number of cases has not. There are still innumerable examples of companies taking a rather unusual view of what is extraordinary. It seems that the 'try it on the chairman and see what he says' method is alive and well and living in boardrooms everywhere.

Take the 1985/86 interim results from CASE, the computer company. It had not been having a good year and it reported pre-tax losses of £3.4 million for the half-year compared with a pre-tax profit of £4.2 million at the same stage a year earlier. However, this reported loss was flattered by the inclusion above the line of an exceptional profit of £2 million from the sale of a US property. The company admitted that this was a one-off item, which would suggest that it should have been classified as extraordinary and thus excluded from CASE's earnings, which would in turn have increased the loss per share.

It was not the only piece of creative presentation in the interim statement. The company also chose to recognise a substantial tax credit relating to US losses. The effect was to reduce the reported after-tax losses by £1.1 million. Again the company indicated that it was not entirely sure about the method of presentation, since it included its own internally generated equivalent of a qualified interim audit report. Referring to the tax credit, CASE said: 'The recognition of this is dependent inter alia upon the results of the group's operations in the US for the second half of the year.' It is not exactly the kind of thing you expect to find in an interim statement and represents a real slap in the face for the accountant's traditional virtue of prudence.

The net effect of these two treatments was to reduce CASE's reported after-tax losses by £3 million to £2.2 million. *The Times* was moved to comment: 'The CASE interim profit and loss account has been constructed with all the finesse of a bulldozer. The accounting is so creative that it probably merits a grant from the Arts Council.' Quite so.

A further example of how to make extraordinary circumstances produce exceptional profits came in the preliminary announcement of results from Greenall Whitley, the regional brewery company, for its year ended 27 September 1985. The company had the misfortune of one of its hotels in the US burning down. Fortunately the insurance premiums were up-to-date and the insurers duly coughed up. The compensation came in two parts. One chunk was to cover the loss of profits while the hotel was out of commission. The second part was to pay for the damage to the building itself which Greenall Whitley repaired and rebuilt.

The loss of profits element was included as part of the

hotel division's operating profit for the year, although the amount was not quantified. However, the capital element of the insurance money amounting to £1.7 million was treated as an exceptional item and disclosed above the line. The justification was that this insurance money was similar in nature to other property sales which are regularly accounted for above the line. Collecting the insurance proceeds on burnt down hotels would not appear to be part of the company's ordinary business. Yet the uncertainty in the accounting rules on the treatment of such proceeds presents a loophole which simply invites companies to take advantage of it.

The battle to introduce some consistency of treatment will last as long as there is one set of accountants setting the rules and another set of accountants trying to implement them in practice. It leaves the auditor rather uncomfortably as the piggy in the middle of this continuing conflict. The best that can be hoped for is that they themselves will be consistent in their approach to this exceptionally extraordinary problem.

However, the opportunities for creative accounting in this area are not merely restricted to distinguishing between what is exceptional and what is extraordinary. The very presence of an extraordinary item of some magnitude offers an excellent opportunity to sweep away a lot of rather unpleasant bad news at one fell swoop. This is what companies like to refer to as 'taking it on the chin' in the time-honoured tradition of maintaining the British stiff upper lip. The reality is slightly different and is most certainly not cricket.

The 'taking it on the chin' approach is most appropriate for companies which clearly have problems, but only ones which are fully appreciated by the stock market and which are already reflected in the share price. Big extraordinary write-offs are well anticipated. In this situation the company has nothing whatsoever to lose by making the extraordinary item as large as possible. Rather than just making provisions and write-offs for the specific extraordinary items, the company provides for all such costs irrespective of when they will be incurred. The name of the game is to recognise all these costs at this early stage and thus avoid the embarrassment of making further provisions at a later date.

By getting all the bad news out of the way the company will then be able to give the impression in subsequent reporting periods that it is making progress and on the way to returning to good health. It is an important psychological factor which will not always reflect the real progression. A company may actually be laying off people a year or two years after the cost of that redundancy was first provided for in the accounts. In 1981/82 British Airways charged £198.4 million below the line, of which nearly half related to future job losses. In later years part of that provision was written back.

This subtle deception is only part of the story. For by making the extraordinary write-offs and provisions as large and far-sighted as possible a company will be able to take below the line costs which in the normal run of events have been taken above the line as exceptional items. It is very difficult when assessing provisions which are perhaps based on a two-year plan for the company, which could involve rationalisation, re-organisation, closures and disposals, to say with any certainty how accurate those provisions are, let alone whether the costs involved are extraordinary or exceptional.

The temptation will be to treat everything as extra-ordinary, although some token but small exceptional items might be thrown in for credibility purposes, and thus mitigate the impact on earnings. Once these massive provisions have been created the actual costs incurred will be written off directly to them and will then not spoil the appearance of a profit and loss account, which from being horribly scarred in one year becomes totally unblemished the next. This com-bination of subtle presentation and astute timing can be devastating.

Take two companies in the same industry. Both have suffered from the impact of the recession and therefore decide to introduce a series of measures to put their businesses back on an even keel. Company A estimates the cost of the rational-isation programme will be £100 million over three years and takes this as an extraordinary item in year 1. Company B decides to account for the cost of the restructuring as and when specific closure decisions are taken and will account for them in accordance with the rules of extraordinary and exceptional items. The trading results of the companies are identical over the three-year period. No tax is payable.

	Year 1		Year 2		Year 3	
	A	B	A	B	A	B
	£m	£m	£m	£m	£m	£m
Trading Profit/(loss)	(10)	(10)	5	5	15	15
Exceptional item (restructuring)	—	(10)	—	(10)	—	(10)
Restructuring provision no longer needed, written back	—	—	—	—	10	—
Profits/(losses) attributable to shareholders	(10)	(20)	5	(5)	25	5
Extraordinary item (restructuring)	(100)	(20)	—	(20)	—	(20)
Transfer to/(from) reserves	(110)	(40)	5	(25)	25	(15)

Over the three-year period the net cost which has to be deducted from reserves amounts to £80 million for both companies being the £90 million actual cost of restructuring less net trading profits of £10 million.

The benefit for company A of taking the restructuring costs on the chin is quite considerable. Its profits attributable to shareholders, which determine earnings per share, show a steady recovery from the initial loss in year 1, while company B does not show an attributable profit until year 3. The decision to take a particular approach will be determined by the amount of distributable reserves which each company has. It is out of these reserves that a company pays its dividends to shareholders. The assumption is that Company A has substantial reserves which will allow it to carry on paying dividends. Without those, dividend payments may have to be withheld, which does little for stock market confidence in the company. However, the decision on which method to adopt will take these factors into account.

By treating all the costs as an extraordinary item at the outset, a company affords itself a much greater control over its reported figures. Once again a prime objective is to produce a smooth and steady progression of profits and earnings growth. The stock market does not like wild fluctuations in profits. Consistency is the name of the game, but in playing by the stock market's rules, companies are obliged to abandon the rules of consistency imposed by the accountancy profession. By breaking these rules and taking an inconsistent view on what is extraordinary and what is exceptional, a business can bring an element of smoothing to its results. It will not always be expedient to take all the bad news below the line and the good news above. There may be occasions when a company would prefer to reduce its reported profits for a particular year and it therefore treats unusual items accordingly. This may manifest itself as some redundancy costs being taken above the line or perhaps a property disposal, another favourite for loose interpretation of the rules, being treated as an extraordinary item and disclosed below the line. An example of this clever presentation came from the Granada Group's preliminary announcement of results for the 52 weeks ended 28 September 1985. The company, best known for its TV contracting business which makes Coronation Street but which also has other wide interests, reported pre-tax profits of £64.4 million up from £53.8 million. A reasonable 20 per cent increase in itself but one which could have been much higher if the company had chosen to take a £6.5 million profit on the disposal of one of its properties above the line as well.

Instead, Granada decided to report it below the line and netted it off against a £4.1 million extraordinary loss on the sale of its troubled insurance businesses. The group therefore disclosed an extraordinary gain of just £2.4 million. The effect of this approach is twofold. First it masks the loss which had been made on the insurance business. Second it results in a much lower base from which to increase profits in 1985/86. The City analysts forecast a 25 per cent increase from the group to £80 million for that year. Had that percentage increase been applied to profits of £71 million which Granada would have reported if it had taken the profit on the property sale above the line, then the brokers' forecasts would have been closer to £88 million. Given the importance for companies of meeting those forecasts, it becomes clear that Granada now has a much greater margin for error and is much better placed to produce a steady growth rate in its profits.

The treatment adopted by Granada also highlights a further area of exploitation which is available to the creative accountant, that of netting off. This approach is particularly useful at a company's interim or preliminary reporting stage. These are the key times for the stock market analysts who tend to focus more attention on these figures than on the annual accounts which are published some weeks after the preliminary announcement of full year results has been made. The scope for disguising netting off is more limited in the accounts since the accounting rules dictate that an analysis of the components which go to make the single figure for extraordinary items disclosed in the profit and loss and account, be produced by way of a note to the accounts.

However, since preliminary and interim announcements of results are not subject to audit, those disclosure requirements need not be met. A company is therefore able to disguise big extraordinary losses by setting them off against big extra-ordinary gains. It is hardly the most subtle of tactics but one which can be effective. There is no doubt that a large extra-ordinary item attracts more attention than a small one which is dismissed, normally quite rightly, as being immaterial. A below the line charge of £20 million will be seized upon while one of £20,000 might well go unchallenged. Yet that £20,000 may be the net effect of a £20.2 million loss on write-downs at a major division less a £20 million profit on the sale of a property. Those write-downs are critical to forming a clear and full understanding of the business yet, unless the company volunteers the information at the preliminary or interim stage, then there is no reason why observers should find out about it.

While extraordinary items offer perhaps the greatest scope for improving the presentation of figures they do not have the monopoly on the subject. There are other ways of puffing up the profit and loss account simply by setting out and treating the same item in a variety of ways. One area which is eminently suited to such an approach is that of associated companies. These are businesses in which the parent has a substantial investment but does not have absolute control since the stake is under 50 per cent.

The accounting rules that govern which investments should be granted associate or related company status once again are open to various interpretations. They recognise that there is a different underlying principle for holding an investment in a company merely for trading purposes and for holding a substantial investment for the long term. A trade investment might be merely a way for a company to make use of surplus cash for which it has no immediate need, with the return coming in the shape of dividends and capital growth which will be realised on disposal. The much larger investments which typify an associate company imply that it forms part of a long term strategy with the intention of sharing more fully in its fortunes.

However, it follows that the distinction between what is an associate and what is a trade investment must be made on a purely arbitrary basis, since hard and fast rules would not allow for the varying commercial and business situations which affect different arrangements. It is this which permits a parent company some flexibility of presentation.

The distinction embodied in Statement of Standard Accounting Practice 1 (SSAP 1) which deals with associated companies is based on the view that an investing company participates actively in the commercial and policy decisions of its associated companies. It thus has a measure of direct responsibility for the return on its investment and should account for its stewardship accordingly. However, it will not seek to exert direct management influence over the operating policy of other companies which are treated as trade investments. In practical profit and loss terms this distinction means that for trade investments the holding company takes credit only for the dividends it receives which are disclosed as part of investment income. For associated companies, however, the holding company is entitled to take credit for its share of profits or losses of the entire business in its own profit and loss account. It would also reflect post acquisition retained profits or losses in its balance sheet.

The effect of the different treatments can be quite material. The share of profits from an associated company would be much larger than just the dividends actually paid over. Similarly the impact of losses is much greater than an absence of dividend payments.

The definition of an associated company set out in SSAP 1 is one in which the interest of the investing company is effectively that of a partner in a joint venture or consortium where it is in a position to exercise a significant influence over the company in which the investment is made. However, there is an optional definition which is the source of the flexibility of treatment.

This states that the interest of the investing group should be for the long term and substantial. Also, with due regard to the disposition of other shareholdings, the investing group should be in a position, again, to exercise a significant influence over the company if it is to be treated as an associate. There is further amplification of 'significant influence' which essentially involves participation, not control, of financial and operating policy decisions. Representation on the board of directors is a strong indication of such participation but is not in itself conclusive. In terms of guidance on what is a substantial investment SSAP 1 suggests that when the holding company is entitled to 20 per cent or more of the voting rights in the associate then it should be assumed that 'significant influence' can be exerted. Only if the holding company has a stake of more than 20 per cent but can demonstrate that it does not have that influence, should the investment be given trade rather than associate status. Conversely, if the investment amounts to less than 20 per cent of the voting rights it should be treated as trade in nature unless it can be proved otherwise.

This is all well and good but it is apparent from these definitions that 'significant influence' is far from clearly spelt out. Whenever a company is asked to demonstrate something it is a guarantee that it will come up with the evidence which proves beyond a shadow of a doubt that it can proceed with the treatment which suits it best. A further problem comes from the assumption implicit in the accounting standard that any stake above 20 per cent is an associate and anything below is not. What becomes, for instance, of a 19.999 recurring per cent investment?

The problem of significant control is at its most acute during take-over bid battles. The unwelcome predator will often signal its interest and bid by acquiring a substantial stake in the target company which it may then increase during the course of the take-over often to more than the key 20 per cent associate cut-off point. The question then is, how should that stake be treated?

This very difficulty arose during United Newspapers' bid for Fleet Holdings. In this case United had held its stake for some time before the bid finally got going properly. So when it published its own results to demonstrate its financial strength it included a share of Fleet's profits. Clearly this improved United's results, much to the chagrin of the defending Fleet Holdings who found their own profits being used as evidence against them. The Fleet camp argued that United did not exert the significant influence necessary to qualify the holding for associate status. You can see their point. Given that the two companies were in direct conflict it was hardly likely that the Fleet board would treat anything suggested by United with anything other than contempt.

This kind of conflict will crop up with increasing frequency as bid battles are fought using much more sophisticated tactics and weapons than was once the case. However, it is not only during take-over battles that interpretation of the rules becomes important. There will also be an incentive for companies to take advantage of the flexibility of the accounting rules in order to influence the figures produced as part of the normal reporting cycle.

If a company holds a 20 per cent stake in another business which it has treated as an associate but that business runs into difficulties and is likely to produce losses, what is to stop the holding company selling a few shares in the market to take the investment below 20 per cent? Once the stake is less than the magical cut-off point, the holding company need not account for its share of any losses thus improving its own position. If the fortunes of the former associate pick up at a later date, the holding company can go back into the market and buy enough shares to take the investment above 20 per cent again. It is not perhaps the kind of tactic that can be employed too frequently without arousing the auditors' suspicions, but as a short term smoothing measure it could be very effective.

The underlying principle is similar to that of a holding company deciding not to consolidate a subsidiary. Such a decision may appear to conflict directly with the whole concept of group accounting. In theory it does, but there are several circumstances where it is perfectly legitimate for a holding company to exclude the results of a subsidiary from its own accounts.

The situations where exclusion is allowed are set out through a combination of company law and the accounting standard which deals with the preparation of group accounts. Again the rules appear to be fairly clearly defined, but their wording is sufficiently vague for a company to apply a variety of interpretations which bring opportunities for a little creative thinking.

According to company legislation a subsidiary may be excluded from consolidation where it would be impractical or of no real value; where it would involve disproportionate expense or delay; where inclusion could be harmful or misleading; finally, where the business of the holding company and the subsidiary are so different that they cannot be reasonably treated as a single entity. If any one of these four conditions persists then the subsidiary can be excluded. The accounting rules extend the law and if anything are more restrictive. The standard recognises that dissimilar activities are sufficient grounds for exclusion. It also cites lack of effective control and the situation where control is only intended to be temporary as further reasons for leaving out a subsidiary's results. Finally it permits exclusion where the subsidiary is operating under severe restrictions.

By and large holding companies will tend not to take advantage of these provisions. After all, there is little point in spending a small fortune on getting control of a company only to proceed to leave its results out of the group's figures. However, there are situations where judicious use of the exclusion clauses can be made. It is particularly appropriate for multinationals which by their very nature tend to have a multitude of overseas operations including many in the developing countries. The economic and political uncertainty which is often found in such nations can bring commercial problems for the international holding company. Import restrictions may make it difficult to make capital investment, exchange controls could make repatriation of funds impossible or trading may simply take a turn for the worse.

Whatever the reasons which cause the poor performance, it is clear that the holding company will not be too happy about including heavy losses in its accounts. Exclusion of the entire subsidiary becomes the most appropriate solution. The amount of the holding company's investment in the subsidiary is retained in the consolidated balance sheet, but it should be possible to get away without making any provisions to reflect the local problems. Once the situation has stabilised then the holding company is free to return once again to full consolidation.

BOC Group took advantage of the exclusion provisions in its 1983/84 accounts to exclude the results of its Nigerian subsidiary which was clearly undergoing severe problems, boosting its results for the year into the bargain. But it is not just for practical profits reasons that a company chooses to exclude a subsidiary. Trusthouse Forte, for instance, excluded the results of the Savoy Hotel because, although, as at 31 October 1984 it owned 69 per cent of the equity, this brought it only 42.3 per cent of the voting rights. Effective control is therefore absent. By excluding the Savoy from its figures, ThF not only complies with best accounting practice but at the same time makes a very effective point about the iniquities of the Savoy's share voting structure, which has riled it for so long.

The exclusion of subsidiaries is just another example of

how a company can improve the appearance of its figures merely by subtle presentation. The actual figures are not manipulated, it is the way in which they are set out, or not, in the accounts which brings the creativity.

The principle is extended in another form of lethally creative presentation which goes under the guise of the accounting policies which a company adopts. These are critical in determining the framework within which the figures that go to make up the accounts are calculated. Accounting policies are to the creative accountant what the left hook was to Henry Cooper. Without them they are powerless.

The specific impact of individual policies are dealt with in the relevant chapters but it is clear that, in general, the overriding rule of consistency simply pleads to be broken. Wholesale changes in policy on a regular basis is not what the accountancy profession had in mind when it insisted on consistency. Consistent inconsistency is not on. However, so numerous are the accounting policies which a company uses and so vague their definition that it is possible to make subtle amendments on a fairly regular basis without attracting undue attention.

Again the emphasis is not so much on manipulation of the specific figures to which a policy relates, but more on the treatment which affects the way they appear in the accounts. By using the argument that a change in policy provides a fairer reflection of the company's operations amendments can be made almost at will. Clearly changing the same accounting policy each year, such as switching the average from closing exchange rates and back again for currency translation purposes, would not go down too well. However, if a company so wishes, it can operate a rotating system of changing policies which allows it to achieve the desired effect almost unnoticed.

If the accounting policies prove a little stubborn and will not bend under some gentle manipulation, then there are still some further alternatives. One of the simplest is simply to play around with the captions used in the balance sheet and profit and loss account to describe various items. The new Companies

Acts appear to have restricted the scope for using this ploy but by offering optional presentation formats there is still sufficient opportunity to gloss over some of the more unsavoury aspects of the accounts. By adding certain captions and leaving out others then tossing in some transfers to and from reserves, it can be quite difficult to find out what the directors actually believe is the profit or loss for the year. On the balance sheet one well-known cross-Channel transportation company, faced with the unfortunate prospect of having negative totals on its balance sheet due to an excess of liabilities over assets, simply transferred its long term liabilities to the capital employed, half of the balance sheet thus restoring a more positive outlook.

On a grander scale companies can also change their complete accounting convention. Such a move is rare mainly because companies stick firmly with the historical cost convention. The current cost convention of inflation accounting, which the profession has fought vainly to introduce, never really caught on apart from among the nationalised industries. However, the change in convention becomes particularly pertinent when a company makes the transition from the public to the private sector. This is a more regular occurrence given the Conservative government's commitment to privatisation.

The British Telecom flotation was a prime example of how to switch the accounting convention to great effect. While it was nationalised it had gone along with the government's insistence that current cost accounting was the most appropriate way of preparing its accounts. The same basis was applied to the gas and electricity industries, mainly because current cost accounting has the effect of depressing profits and thus giving the impression that these public utilities are not raking the money in from the unsuspecting and captive public at such an extortionate rate. Ironically, current cost accounting is not deemed quite so appropriate for the less profitable nationalised industries such as coal and steel. They use historical cost accounting because this has the effect of reducing the extent of their losses. It is all very convenient for the industries, but makes it very difficult for the consumer, and indeed the government, to assess whether they are getting a good deal from the industries which serve them.

Returning to Telecom's privatisation, the company had a sudden change of heart over its accounting convention. You can picture the directors sitting around their boardroom table suddenly being hit by a vision not unlike the one that greeted Saul of Tarsus on the Road to Damascus. Just as his conversion was dramatic so too was that of British Telecom: the entire board must have been blinded by the sudden revelation that after all these years it had discovered that it had been using the wrong accounting convention. Much weeping, wailing, gnashing of teeth and smacking of foreheads was no doubt in order as a result of this sad realisation of the error of its ways, but this was soon put right as Telecom announced that it was switching to the historical cost accounting convention.

At a stroke the company was treated to a massive increase in profits. The argument put forward in defence of the change was that the City and its stock market are used to dealing with figures presented under the historical cost convention and a privatised Telecom felt obliged to fall into line with other companies with a Stock Exchange quote. It is hardly the most convincing of arguments. It follows that if current cost accounting is the most appropriate method of preparing the accounts whilst in public ownership, then it must still be the most appropriate even if the company has moved to the private sector. Such blatant manipulation tends to be overlooked, however, in the euphoria of the flotation with investors more concerned about grabbing as many shares as possible in the hope of earning a fat premium, than assessing the fundamental basis on which the company prepares its accounts.

It is not just the nationalised industries which can take advantage of using an accounting convention which is not entirely appropriate. Other companies can do exactly the same but in a way which is potentially more damaging. This is by preparing the accounts on the basis that the company is a going concern when in fact there are doubts about its financial viability. One of the fundamental accounting concepts on which the accountancy profession insists, is that the business must be a going concern; in other words it is not going to go bust the day after the accounts are published.

It is a perfectly reasonable demand. No one comes too well out of a situation where a company goes to the wall. It is therefore sensible for a company which is facing a financial crisis to prepare its accounts in a way which reflects the problems. Unfortunately the company itself may not take the same view. Open admission that it is in difficulties may be the straw that finally breaks its financial back. There is therefore a strong incentive to make the assumption, no matter how misguided, that the company is a going concern. The value which is placed on the assets of the business will be much reduced if the company is fit only for the knackers yard. When a company is broken up its assets will be sold at a price which rarely reflects their economic value to the business. The bargain basement prices which result from an 'everything must go' sale, if reflected in the company's balance sheet, will cast an altogether more unpleasant shadow over the accounts. It is clear then that by adopting the going concern convention, the company will be presenting its figures in a much more favourable fashion.

Hopefully for shareholders, any serious abuse of the going concern convention or doubts about its use will be reflected in the auditors' report. However, the other creative presentation measures which a company has adopted will not always be so clear from the accounts. Once again the creative accountants' meat may turn out to be the shareholders' poison.

6

HOW to TAMPER with TAXATION

*T*here are two items in the profit and loss account which companies generally have a great aversion to paying. One is the audit fee, the other is taxation. Both costs have to be incurred as a result of externally imposed legislation and neither, despite what the auditing profession would have us believe, provide any tangible benefit for the business. Some cynics argue that the audit fee is little more than hush money handed over to the auditor in return for his acquiescence on the more dubious methods of creative accounting. But as any audit junior who has spent endless hours poring over grubby invoices in the bowels of the client's head office will tell you, this is not the case.

Taxation is another matter entirely. It is a price which has to be paid for success. The more you earn, the more tax you pay. This is a fact that most companies have now come to accept but this has not stopped them from doing everything in their power to reduce the amount which will actually have to be paid over to the Inland Revenue. The tax planning industry has boomed in recent years as company accountants and their advisers work out ingenious ways of reducing the figure which will ultimately have to be written on the cheque which will find its way into the Exchequer's coffers.

Tax planning is a huge subject which is reflected in the library of publications which deals with it. Its importance to a company ranks alongside that of creative accounting, but to try and cover the issues in this chapter would not do them justice.

However, there are some more general points which can be usefully examined. After all, there is an inextricable link between a company's profits and the tax which will ultimately be charged on them. Therefore, the creative accounting techniques which are used to influence those profits must always be seen in the context of the tax as well as the stock market implications. One of the country's leading companies and a constituent of the FT 30 stock market index, which shall remain nameless, admits privately that its annual profits are governed entirely by the amount of taxation that it is prepared to pay. In other words, it decides on the cash it will hand over to the government and then constructs its profit and loss account in order to arrive at the desired result. It is clear than that tax planning and creative accounting go hand in hand.

But it is important to remember that the taxman is not easily fooled. He didn't get where he is today by being easily fooled. While many investors seem to have eyes with signs saying 'please pull wool over' the Inland Revenue is a little more discerning in its assessment of the accounts laid before it. Many of the creative accounting adjustments will have to be excluded from the tax computation anyway. It is important then to have an honest and open relationship with the Revenue. This investment in the Inland Revenue's swings will be more than recouped by the returns which a company will subsequently make on the tax planning roundabouts.

This said, there are still some genuine creative accounting points which must be considered in isolation from the physical taxation which must be paid and the planning which is undertaken before that figure is struck. The tax charge as reported in the accounts is in itself extremely important, since it has to be deducted from profits in order to arrive at the earnings which are available for distribution to shareholders. The rate at which tax will be charged to a company's profits is therefore crucial in determining the earnings per share which will be used in calculating the price earnings ratio. The lower the tax charge the more profits there are available for shareholders. This fact has not been lost on those companies which have been able to make up the ground lost on poor profits by a reduction in the reported corporation tax bill.

That figure will normally have been computed on a different basis to the one used for determining the actual corporate tax liability. This stems from the fact that certain types of income will be free of tax and certain expenses incurred by the company will be disallowed as a deduction from taxable profits. Further, there might also be certain tax allowances and charges affecting the total liability which make no corresponding appearance in the published profit and loss account. These items result in 'permanent differences' between accounting profits and taxable profits. Because they are permanent, these differences do not actually bring any specific accounting problems and all that happens is that the tax charge varies from the standard rate of corporation tax, depending on the respective levels of the disallowable expenses and charges and the tax free income and allowances.

However, there will also be some items which will be accounted for and reported in a company's financial statements in an accounting period which is different from the one in which they are dealt with for the purposes of preparing the tax computation. Such items result in 'timing differences'. The tax attributable to these differences goes under the name 'Deferred Taxation'. Statement of Standard Accounting Practice 15, which deals with the subject, defines timing differences as: 'The differences between profits or losses as computed for tax purposes and results as stated in financial statements, which arise from the inclusion of items of income and expenditure in tax computations in periods different from those in which they are included in financial statements. Timing differences originate in one period and are capable of reversal in one or more subsequent periods.'

The main thrust of the accounting standard is that companies should account for this deferred, or in some cases accelerated, taxation to the extent that it is likely to crystallise at some later date. The approach which it advocates as being the most appropriate for accounting for deferred taxation is known as the 'liability method'. Under this approach the tax charge as reported in the accounts is based on the profits disclosed in those accounts. The charge will reflect any permanent differences and those timing differences which are not expected to reverse. The difference between the reported taxation and the actual charge for the year is treated as a future liability and carried forward as such in the balance sheet.

The key to the creative accounting opportunities is the assessment which must be made on whether or not timing differences are expected to reverse and thus crystallise a liability. The ever-virtuous accounting standard informs us that this assessment 'should be based upon reasonable assumptions'. Quite so. But what does reasonable mean? The man on the Clapham omnibus, so often the arbiter on such delicate questions, will know as much about deferred taxation as Idi Amin knew about human rights.

There is some guidance from the standard, not on what is reasonable but on the nature of the assumptions. These should take into account all the relevant information which is available up to the date on which the financial statements are approved by the board of directors. They should also reflect the intentions of management. One assumes this is referring to their intentions on business strategy rather than their intentions to keep the tax charge at rock bottom this year. The guidance in the standard also makes some assumptions of its own and in particular it assumes a perfect world. The suggestion is that the information which is made available should include financial plans or projections covering a period of years sufficient to enable an assessment to be made of the likely pattern of future tax liabilities. In a perfect world and among the larger companies such projections are doubtless available, but given that in some companies the forward planning of the directors is restricted to finding out from their secretaries where they are going for lunch after the board meeting, the chances of these forecasts being widely used must be somewhat limited.

This is acknowledged to a certain extent by the standard which insists that where the financial plans or projections are susceptible to a high degree of uncertainty or are not fully developed for the appropriate period, then a prudent view on the assessment of the liability should be taken. So where the company's five-year plan is written on the back of a betting slip, the best that can be hoped for is that the directors are reasonable and prudent men.

Even if the standard is rather vague it is clear that its spirit is intended to ensure that some detailed consideration is given to the subject. Inevitably it will require an element of subjective judgement which, providing it is supported by an indication that the homework has been studiously completed, should allow the company to make the provision which suits it best.

That homework should take the form of budgets, forecasts, capital expenditure programmes, details of long term strategy and anything else which gives the impression that the company knows exactly what it is doing and where it is going. This may all sound rather grand and detailed which, in theory, it is. But the practical reality is that much of the information should be readily available in respect of the company's immediate plans, and the longer term forecasts will comprise little more than general statements of principles and intentions. Company auditors are well aware of the practical difficulties involved in preparing detailed long term projections and will accept more abbreviated data as an acceptable indication of the business outlook.

The company must also look closely at whether it wants to take advantage of all the tax allowances which often give rise to the timing differences. Generally, the desire to keep the tax charge as low as possible means that those allowances will be used as soon as they become available, although there may be certain circumstances where this is not the case. The company may want to boost taxable profits, perhaps to obtain double taxation relief on overseas earnings or to allow the recovery of Advance Corporation Tax (ACT). It may also want to retain a higher amount of taxable profits than is strictly necessary in order to take advantage of the group taxation relief provisions.

The view that the company takes on the level of the provision it should make for deferred taxation will be coloured by the overall reported rate which it wants to include in its accounts. Any increase in the provision will increase the charge for the year but this may be written back at a later date on the grounds that it is no longer needed, thus reducing the rate of charge in that subsequent year.

The stock market acknowledges the effects of deferred taxation by looking at both the actual reported position and also that which would result if tax was charged at the full rate. This gives two different price earnings multiples, although it has to be said that the one using the actual tax basis tends to be more popular. Given the importance of those multiples in assessing a share price, there is a temptation for the company to manipulate the amounts of deferred tax it charges or releases in a particular year in order to influence its earnings.

The tax charge for the year is also influenced by ACT which is the amount a company effectively hands over to the government when it makes a dividend payment to shareholders. That ACT is available to be offset against the mainstream tax liability as and when this falls due. In theory it is a deferred asset which can be used to reduce the deferred tax liability. However, just as the company must produce the evidence to suggest that a liability will not crystallise, it also has to produce evidence which supports the assessment that the ACT is in fact recoverable. Given the success with which many companies manage to avoid their mainstream tax liabilities, it might be difficult to argue that any surplus ACT is recoverable in the short term. The very clever companies manage to ensure that the corporation tax they have to pay is matched exactly by their ACT which gets round the problem. However, where this is not the case, it could be difficult to justify carrying the surplus forward and it therefore has to be written off as part of the charge for the year as irrecoverable.

As might be expected in this complex area, irrecoverable doesn't mean that the ACT cannot be recovered. It means that the ACT cannot be recovered the next year without being replaced by a further surplus. So by making the write off the company is effectively building up a hidden asset, which can be brought into play whenever a mainstream corporation tax liability arises. That unrelieved ACT is simply used to offset the mainstream liability, thus reducing the reported charge in a particular year.

Further opportunities for creativity come in the shape of the group taxation relief provisions which enable losses in one subsidiary to be offset against the profits of another. These provisions also allow ACT paid by the parent to be surrendered down to its subsidiaries. Once more, before a company is able to take advantage of these provisions, it might be required to furnish evidence to support its claim that it is entitled so to do. The interpretation of the group's affairs and prospects with respect to group relief may allow the company to reduce the amount of deferred taxation which it has to provide, thus again restricting the tax charge in a particular year.

The tax planning considerations are perhaps, in this area, more important than those of creative accounting. There is no doubt that the group structure offers tremendous scope for reducing the overall liability to corporation tax, particularly when it is also considered alongside the overseas tax arrangements and the relief which is available for double taxation. Any company which does not pay careful attention to tax management has more money than sense. The creative accounting opportunities with regard to tax are much more appropriate for smoothing out the short term fluctuations in the charge. However, the efforts made in that direction will be undermined if the tax affairs in the real world have not been planned efficiently and effectively. Once the genuine tax liabilities which have to be handed over in hard cash to the Inland Revenue begin to rise and perhaps get a little out of hand, the task of reducing these to a more acceptable level, for the purposes of disclosure in the annual accounts, becomes that much harder.

7

HOW to FIDDLE FOREIGN CURRENCY TRANSLATION

Although the British have traditionally been an island race, few companies these days can afford to accept this as a fact of commercial life and take comfort from the reassurance that this provides. Instead, most businesses actively strive to broaden their trading horizons. This involves, in its simplest form, either exporting finished products or importing goods for reprocessing or onward sale. The more advanced international traders will have subsidiaries and investments based overseas. Whatever the nature and magnitude of a company's international business, it will at some stage have to deal with the vagaries of the foreign exchange markets. A transaction which appears quite profitable at one exchange rate will suddenly plunge into loss at another. An overseas investment can have its value eroded as exchange rates change.

The exposure to currency fluctuations is a price that has to be paid for access to international markets. Of course that price can often result in a very welcome refund if exchange rates reverse, as they often will, on the principle that what goes up must come down, even if it does go up again at a later date. Clearly the erratic nature of exchange rates is something of a problem. It is yet another uncertainty with which a business has to cope when it is trying to plan its longer term strategy and assess investment opportunities. In recent years currency movements appear to have become even more frequent and pronounced. As the process of internationalisation of capital markets gains momentum, and currency speculators take advantage of the new opportunities which present themselves, the prospects for stabilisation will become even more remote. However, it is not just the practical trading uncertainties which pose problems for a company. Some of these can be offset anyway by some judicious hedging. A more lasting difficulty is over how to deal with the surpluses and deficits which arise when overseas assets and liabilities denominated in foreign currencies are translated back into sterling for consolidation purposes. It is a difficulty which has been recognised by the accountancy profession and its rules on how to translate the financial statements of foreign subsidiaries are set out in Statement of Standard Accounting Practice 20 (SSAP 20). As usual the rules appear to be fairly rigid but in fact offer an element of flexibility.

The basic rules for translating the results of foreign subsidiaries are that a company should use the 'closing rate/net investment' method. This recognises that the parent's investment is not in the individual assets and liabilities of an overseas company but rather in its net worth. This is represented, in effect, by the equity stake which the parent has in the foreign company's net assets. Under this translation method, the parent should apply the closing rate of exchange, that is the rate in force at the balance sheet date, when translating its net investment in the foreign subsidiary. This process also involves retranslation of the net investment at the beginning of the year at the exchange rate used at the year end. This will normally give rise to an exchange difference, which could be either a profit or a loss. That difference does not have to be reflected in the consolidated profit and loss account but instead is taken direct to the group reserves and disclosed as a movement thereon.

The parent must also consolidate the actual trading results of the overseas subsidiary and here the accounting rules permit two different methods of translation. The holding company can choose either to use the closing exchange rate or an average for the year. If it chooses the average rate then this can be calculated on any reasonable basis although it should be weighted to reflect the changes both in the exchange rate itself and the volume of transactions at particular times of year. It is this option on which rate to use for the translation exercise which presents an immediate creative accounting opportunity and one which has been grasped gleefully by innumerable companies in recent months. There has been a regular stream of announcements from companies which have decided that the time has come for them to switch from using the closing rate to the average rate of exchange for translating the results of overseas subsidiaries. This sudden change of heart has largely been influenced by the dramatic change in the fortunes of sterling's performance against the dollar. At the end of 1984 it was in decline and heading for parity. By the end of 1985 it had recovered and was hovering around the $1.45 mark.

The financial effect of that change is best illustrated by a simple example. Take a US subsidiary which makes profits of $10 million in both 1984 and 1985. The year end translation rates are taken as $1.1 and $1.4 respectively to the pound. In 1984 the sterling equivalent of the US profit is around £9.1 million. But at 1985 closing exchange rates the same profit in dollar terms is reduced to a little over £7.1 million, a £2 million fall.

This, of course, has not gone down too well with company chairmen up and down the country who quite rightly want to know why reported profits have gone down when in reality they have stayed the same. Long orations on the injustices of the foreign exchange markets are no response to falling profits, so enter stage left the average exchange rate. Using the example above and assuming that the average is $1.2 to the pound, the $10 million profit then becomes on translation a sterling profit of £8.3 million. It is still a fall but not nearly as exaggerated as the one which is reported using the closing rate.

The arguments which are often presented in defence of the change in the exchange rate used in translation are well rehearsed. The average is more representative of the actual rates ruling during the year. This method reflects more closely the underlying trading performance of the individual subsidiary.

The closing rate is rather artificial since it is representative of only one day's dealings in the various exchange markets. This is all true. But the question which must then be asked is 'If it is so right to use average rates now, why were closing rates used in the first place?' The honest answer is that it made reported profits look that much better. Perhaps more instructive than looking at the companies which have switched to average exchange rates is to examine those which have stuck with the closing rate. It is perhaps an indication that their underlying profits in the year have fared better than those of the companies which made the switch. They therefore have the luxury of the switch still in reserve and this can be brought into action in a subsequent period when the going is a little rougher. Redland, for instance, added £3 million to its profits by switching to average exchange rates in 1985, which eased the company's profits up to £108 million and into line with the stock market's expectations. Rank Hovis McDougall increased its profits by £2.7 million with a similar switch for the year ended 31 August 1985 and helped the group's profits up to £71.5 million. BOC, however, despite taking a battering on both the US and Australian dollar, maintained its end rate policy.

A survey of 170 large listed companies by stockbrokers Phillips & Drew in November 1985 revealed that 59 per cent used the year end rate for translation purposes. However, 13 companies had changed to the average rate in the previous two years and a further 10 planned to make a similar switch.

The translation switch has been the most obvious foreign currency ploy used by creative accountants of late, but there is a more subtle tactic which often escapes unnoticed. This relates to the treatment of borrowings, or, in rarer circumstances, deposits. The accounting rules distinguish between short term money, which falls due within one year of the balance sheet date, and long term money. The rules for short term borrowings are that any gains or losses on exchange should be accounted for through the profit and loss account. The short term nature of the funds should allow the company justifiably to treat the gains as realised and thus there will be no conflict with company law which dictates that only those profits which are realised at the balance sheet date should be included in the profit and loss account.

However, the same cannot be said for long term borrowings. Clearly if gains on such borrowings were to be treated as profits then this would conflict with the provisions of company law. The implication of the legal requirements is that any exchange losses would be recognised and accounted for as a deduction from profits for the year, but any gains would have to be excluded until such time as they were realised. This, the accountancy profession says, is illogical and, worse than that, would not comply with the accruals concept. Further, it would also inhibit fair measurement of the performance of the enterprise in the year. For these reasons the accounting standard advocates that exchange gains as well as losses should be recognised in the profit and loss account. This departure from the law must be noted in the accounts, and specific details of gains and losses relating to each item must be maintained. That is a small price to pay for the privilege and few companies which have taken advantage of this anomaly would argue with SSAP 20 which tells us: 'This symmetry of treatment recognises that there will probably be some interaction between currency movements and interest rates and reflects more accurately in the profit and loss account the true results of currency involvement.' Quite so.

However, the accountancy profession giveth and the accountancy profession taketh away. For although the standard openly condones and encourages this outbreak of lawlessness, it does temper its incitement to riot with some words of caution on what it calls the exceptional circumstances, when the gains have got a little large and there are doubts about the convertibility or marketability of the currency in question. It is up to the company to express those doubts so effectively that it can choose to exclude some element of exchange gains should it so wish. This allows it to retain control over the level of reported profit in a particular year which will help to maintain a smooth growth pattern.

The creative accounting opportunities on long term

borrowings do not stop there. Further scope comes in the shape of the treatment of borrowings which have been used to either finance or provide a hedge against foreign equity investments. You will recall that these equity investments must be translated at closing rates of exchange. The differences which arise on the retranslation of the opening net investment at those closing rates are taken directly to and disclosed as a movement on reserves.

The standard permits a similar treatment for those long term borrowings which were taken out as financing or hedging instruments for the overseas investment. This does not in itself seem particularly outrageous and would appear to make a lot of sense. Isn't the matching of assets and liabilities, after all, sound commercial practice? In situations where this has been the genuine motive for raising the overseas borrowings, this is indeed the case. However, this is not always so. Many companies now raise money overseas purely as a function of effective treasury and risk management. Loan portfolios are becoming increasingly diverse as companies make use of the international capital markets and the ever-increasing range of funding instruments which are available. There then arises a problem in identifying which particular loans have been used to finance or hedge against specific overseas investments. The responsibility for that identification rests with the company, and it is well within the realms of possibility that Yen denominated loans taken out in Japan could be designated as hedging instruments against an equity investment in the US. Any losses on the translation of the loan into sterling, which would otherwise have been deducted from profits for the year, can thus be taken direct to reserves and offset instead against the exchange gains on the translation of the equity investment. The opportunities for manipulation are therefore substantial and, although the standard insists on consistency of treatment one year with the next, this will not always be quite so easy to enforce. When borrowings are classified as hedging rather financing instruments, there is little to prevent the company switching into different currencies each year and perpetuating the creativity.

The effect of this flexibility is demonstrated by two companies A and B which both make investments in subsidiaries in Katanga, a small country somewhere in Africa. The net value of both investments at the start of the year is 400 million Katanganese dollars and at that time the exchange rate is 4 to the pound. At the same time, as part of their treasury management programme, both companies take out borrowings in selected currencies from around the world, including a loan in Howhi, a small country in the far east. Both loans are to the value of 600 million Howhian francs and the exchange rate at the start of the year is 6 to the pound. A year later the net investment in Katanga is unchanged but the exchange rate has slipped to 2 to the pound. The Howhian loan in also unchanged but the rate there at the year end is 4 to the pound. Company A decides that the Howhian loan was a hedge against the investment in Katanga and therefore sets the exchange loss on those borrowings against the gain on the investment. Company B treats the Howhian as a long term loan and accounts for it accordingly. The impact of the two different treatments on reserves is as follows.

	Company A		Company B	
	£m	£m	£m	£m
Opening investment				
K$400m at 4	100		100	
Closing investment				
K$400m at 2	200		200	
Exchange gain		100		100
Opening loan				
Hf600m at 6	100		100	
Closing loan				
Hf600m at 4	150		150	
Exchange loss		(50)		—
Net gain taken to				
reserves		50		100

The impact on the company profit and loss accounts, assuming that both A and B made profits of £30 million before exchange adjustments and that no tax is payable, is as follows.

	Company A	Company B
	£m	£m
Trading profits	30	30
Exchange loss	—	(50)
Pre tax profit/(loss)	30	(20)

The overall effect is quite material. By offsetting its exchange loss on the loan against the non-distributable gains on the overseas investment, Company A has kept its trading profits intact. Company B, however, is faced with a loss for the year which of course would not go down too well with the stock market. However, there is a further, important discrepancy which relates to the dividend policies which the two companies are able to pursue. Assuming that neither company has sufficient distributable reserves on which to call, Company B is unable to make a distribution to its shareholders, another bear point as far as the City would be concerned. Company A, however, has profits in the year which are available for distribution and could duly declare a dividend. Yet that dividend is sourced only because Company A adopted a particular accounting treatment. It is a far from satisfactory outcome for not only is comparability between the two companies drastically impaired, but one of them is in a position to embark on a dividend distribution policy which is far from prudent and might in the longer term leave its resources dangerously stretched.

This cross-border classification scheme can, of course, be expanded. A company can actually take out borrowings in countries where interest rates are low, which benefits earnings per share and then deals with any exchange losses through reserves. Similarly a company may decide to transfer, nominally not physically, certain fixed assets out of a subsidiary in a country where the currency is falling into another subsidiary in a country where the currency is rising.

The best that the accountancy profession has to offer on this delicate question is that where a dividend can be paid only because of the offset of an exchange loss on borrowings against a gain on an equity investment, then it may be appropriate to seek legal advice. Some might argue that in these circumstances, psychiatric treatment might be more appropriate.

This illustration is, of course, an extreme example of the impact of different approaches to currency fluctuations, but it does show that within the morass of translations and conversions which have to be undertaken then, there is adequate scope for considerable manipulation. The disclosure requirements relating to foreign currency translation and the complex nature of the transactions and their underlying concepts are such that much of the creative accounting will be hidden from public view. It is very difficult for readers of a set of accounts to appreciate with any degree of certainty, exactly what has been going on.

That obscurity only serves to encourage the use of the techniques which have been outlined above. In general they should only be used for genuine hedging against exchange fluctuations, but the arguments for making use of their profit smoothing propensities are compelling and, providing they are applied in moderation, should not inflict any lasting damage on the company's underlying financial strength.

8

HOW to GET AROUND GOODWILL

*G*oodwill, contrary to public opinion, is not some-thing which comes along with peace towards all men at Christmas time. It is in fact one of the clearest examples of why creative accounting was created. Goodwill, you see, does not really exist. It is what is described, with much wink-ing and tapping of noses, as an intangible asset. Goodwill is a bit like the wind, you cannot see it or hold it but you know it is there. Unfortunately, goodwill is also something of an afterthought.

The need for goodwill stems from the accountancy pro-fession's slavish devotion to the principle that for every debit there should be an equal and opposite credit. It is a principle which has stood accountants in good stead for many years. However, it came under the severest of pressure with the growth of take-overs, particularly those where the purchase price was well in excess of the assets which were actually being bought.

Take a company which has net assets of £10 million. To encourage the owners to sell, a rival business offers £20 million for it. The offer is one that cannot be refused but rapidly dis-integrates into one which cannot be understood once the accountants become involved. They suddenly find themselves in the terrible position where the debits no longer equal the credits. Outcome, misery.

There has to be a credit of £20 million for the purchase

price either in the shape of extra borrowings or a reduction in cash, but this is matched by a debit worth only £10 million, being the acquired company's net assets. Masterfully creative accounting introduces a balancing item, which, for the sake of convenience and professional reputation, shall be called goodwill. By magic the missing £10 million of debits is provided and the sanctity of double entry bookkeeping is preserved.

The only problem with this solution to the difficulty is that it is totally removed from the real trading world. Goodwill is something which exists only in the mind. The profession accepted this, in part, by insisting that the asset be described as intangible. It might be true that a business can build up goodwill amongst its customers either through a reputation for quality or service or reliability. To argue that this goodwill deserves to have a value put on it, however, seems a bit silly since that value is already reflected in customers returning again and again rather than going elsewhere. Indeed the goodwill is only in the eye of the customer and it is he who decides what value to place on it by deciding whether or not to maintain the business relationship.

The theoretical arguments to support the concept of goodwill can therefore be seen to be tenuous in the first place. So tenuous, in fact, that no sooner, it seemed, had goodwill been created than the profession set about arguing over how it should be removed from company accounts altogether.

With such an excellent pedigree it is small wonder that, once the accountancy profession had decided that goodwill should be written off by companies, then accounting methods were promptly devised to get around this unfortunate encumbrance in the nicest possible way. The creative accountant's task was made that much easier: firstly by being given a choice on whether goodwill should be written off immediately to reserves or over a period of time by amortisation through the profit and loss account; secondly, and more importantly, the profession conveniently provided a loophole which made it possible for the goodwill not to arise in the first place. On the grounds that prevention is better than cure this loophole suddenly became much sought-after.

It came in the shape of Statement of Standard Accounting Practice 23, issued by the ASC which deals with the treatment to be adopted in order to account for mergers and acquisitions. It became immediately apparent that there was big difference between accounting for a genuine merger and accounting for an acquisition or take-over. There were tremendous advantages for a company using merger accounting principles. Those advantages were well-founded according to the underlying theory which dictated that the genuine and harmonious joining together of two businesses should be treated differently from a take-over, which might well have been hostile in nature and where the underlying intention may not necessarily have been a simple pooling of resources. Rules were duly laid down, setting out what could be considered a merger and anything which did not comply with these would be deemed a take-over. Rules, though, are made to be broken.

The advantages of merger accounting are demonstrated through a simple example. Company A offers to acquire the entire share capital of Company B. The terms are: one Company A share worth £10 for each of Company B's one million shares. The offer values Company B at £10 million. It has net assets stated in the books at their value of £8 million, with £2 million, therefore, attributable to goodwill. Before the acquisition takes effect the summarised balance sheets of the two companies are as follows:

	Company A £m	Company B £m
Share Capital (£1 shares)	2	1
Distributable Reserves	10	7
	12	8
Net Assets	12	8

The offer is accepted by shareholders in Company B and the two companies become as one. However, the new, enlarged Company A's balance sheet will look very different depending on whether merger or acquisition accounting principles are used. The nature and underlying assets of the combined business is exactly the same, but the presentation of the balance sheets is rather different. That difference is clearly shown in the illustration, below, which shows how Company A shapes up under the two accounting methods:

	Acquisition Accounting £m	Merger Accounting £m
Share Capital (£1 shares)	3	3
Distributable Reserves	10	17
Non-Distributable reserves: Share premium	9	—
	22	20
Goodwill	2	—
Net Assets	20	20
	22	20

There are two immediately apparent differences between the two methods. First, under merger accounting, no goodwill is created and therefore there is no need to write it off, thus either protecting reserves or avoiding an annual deduction for amortisation in the profit and loss account. Second, the distributable reserves are immediately enlarged under merger accounting which may be very useful for a company which is short of retained earnings out of which to pay a dividend. There is a third advantage to merger accounting which is not immediately apparent from the balance sheet. This is that all of Company B's profits for the year of the merger would be available for distribution irrespective of the date of the link-up. Under acquisition accounting only post-acquisition profits can be treated as profit for the year. Thus you can get 365 days' worth of profits for just one day of ownership.

Given the considerable benefits from the use of merger accounting, the accountancy profession might reasonably have been expected to lay down some pretty rigorous rules about when the method could be used: on the surface they appeared to be so. The thrust of the accounting standard was that merger accounting was only appropriate where the consideration given for the target company did not result in substantial resources leaving the group. This was embodied in four main conditions which had to be met in order for merger accounting to be used.

The business combination has to result from a single offer to all holders of equity shares and to all holders of voting shares. As a result of the offer the acquiring company must secure at least 90 per cent of each class of the target company's equity shares and, at the same time, secure 90 per cent of voting rights. Immediately before the offer is made the acquiring company must not own 20 per cent or more of the target company's equity shares or votes. Finally, at least 90 per cent of the consideration must be in the form of equity capital.

The rules seemed clear enough and were sufficiently tough to ensure that only genuine mergers were allowed the privilege of adopting the beneficial accounting procedures. For a short time the creative accountants were stumped. The main problem was that the shareholders in the target companies were not always willing to swap their paper for somebody else's paper. They did not want more shares, they wanted ready cash: this of course would result in the implementation of the less advantageous acquisition accounting principles.

Necessity, however, was soon to prove once more to be the mother of invention. Rescue came in the shape of two imaginative schemes: vendor placing and vendor rights. These schemes allowed acquisition-hungry businesses to comply with and take advantage of the strict form of the merger accounting rules, and at the same time make ready cash available for those shareholders in the target company who were on the brink of selling the family silver.

The vendor placing was the first scheme to appear on the scene. It follows the basic principles of merger accounting in that the offer for the target company is in the form of shares. However, the acquiring company arranges, through its financial adviser — normally a merchant bank — for some if not all of those shares to be placed, usually with institutional investors. Those shareholders in the target company who want cash rather than paper then pass their shares in the acquiring company to the merchant bank in return for the money raised through the placing. The result is that everyone gets exactly what they want. The acquiring company can use merger accounting; shareholders in the target company take their cash; the institutional investors increase their stake in the acquiring company at a reduced price, and the merchant bank gets a nice fat fee. The only loser is the accounting standard which is yet another innocent victim of the legal form of the transaction taking precedent over its practical substance.

Given that there were so many winners from the vendor placing scheme it was not surprising that the cries of 'foul' were somewhat muted. However, there was one objection to the scheme which won considerable support. Ironically, the complaint had nothing to do with the fact that the vendor placing rode roughshod over the spirit of the accounting standard. Rather, it was made on behalf of existing shareholders in the acquiring company and particularly the smaller private shareholders. They were being deprived of any participation in the merger and in fact their interest in the company was being diluted, since the placing shares were offered to institutional investors. The creative accountants could not afford something like this to get in the way of the quest for merger accounting. Another scheme was called for which would placate existing shareholders and at the same time comply with the letter of the accounting standard.

It was soon found, and was simply a variation on the vendor placing theme called vendor rights. The principles are the same as in a vendor placing. The offer for the target company is once again made in shares. The financial adviser again agrees to act as broker to those shareholders who want cash by finding buyers for the acquiring company's shares. However, as part of the placing arrangements the acquiring company's shareholders are given the option to buy back some of the shares offered, as consideration for the purchase on a ratio determined by their existing shareholdings. Once again everyone is very happy, this time existing shareholders included, since they now participate fully in the enlarged company.

The benefits of the vendor rights scheme were clearly illustrated when it was used by the British computer consultancy, Systems Designers International (SDI), to acquire a US software company called Warrington in February 1985. There were two main problems for SDI. The purchase price of £23.5 million was well in excess of Warrington's net assets and the consequent goodwill would have been too large to be absorbed by SDI's reserves. Secondly, the US shareholders were not overly keen to accept shares in a USM quoted company as the purchase consideration and wanted cash. On the surface it seemed then that the deal would be stymied. The need to pay for Warrington in cash meant that acquisition accounting, with its goodwill problems, would have to be used.

The way round this dilemma was a vendor rights issue. SDI issued shares to its merchant banker, Samuel Montagu, which in turn offered them to SDI's shareholders. Those who didn't want the additional shares sold their rights and this stock was placed with institutions. The cash raised by this vendor rights issue was then, in effect, handed over by Samuel Montagu to Warrington's shareholders. Everybody was happy: SDI got Warrington without creating goodwill, the Warrington shareholders got the cash they wanted and SDI shareholders suffered no dilution of their investment. Further, the rights discount using this scheme was only 9 per cent against the market norm of around 20 per cent and the cash was made available immediately rather than after the usual three-week gap.

Both vendor placings and vendor rights are classic examples of creative accounting. They comply completely with the letter of the relevant rules yet at the same time contradict the spirit of those rules to allow the perpetrators to achieve their desired effect. It is easy to point the finger of accusation at those who designed these schemes and blame them for this flagrant abuse of accounting standards. However, if the blame is to be apportioned, then a large chunk of it must lie with those who created a standard which was both spineless and ineffective. The harsh fact of the matter is that the ASC was aware of these avoidance schemes when it put the final seal of approval on its rule on mergers and acquisitions. The choice was between a further delay in introducing the standard while a more effective version was constructed, or opting for the easy way out and publishing rules which were hardly worth the paper they were written on.

With such accommodating attitudes prevalent among the standard setters, it is hard for the individual auditing firms to try and put pressure on their clients to adopt a spiritually uplifting approach to their affairs. Obviously, when the advantages of merger accounting are so blatant it becomes very difficult for an auditor to take offence at the abuse of the rules. After all, that abuse is perfectly legal and the rules of commercial competition dictate that the auditor's services are not indispensable. There is always a long queue of other firms which would be prepared to take an altogether more relaxed view of the issue. The argument that 'everyone else is doing it so why don't we?' suddenly becomes very compelling.

Running with the crowd is not in itself a sufficient motive for bending the rules in order to take advantage of the benefits of merger accounting. This approach will normally be inspired by some other reason, perhaps to enhance the trading performance of a business. The confusion which merger accounting can cause was clearly illustrated in the recent take-over battle which saw Dee Corporation bidding, in the end unsuccessfully, for Booker McConnell. Dee's accounting policies on some of its acquisitions prompted Booker to make a stinging attack.

In its defence document of 14th March 1985 Booker said: 'Dee has what appears to be a good record. It has forecast 1984/85 profits double those of 1983/84. But Dee's forecast and record raise serious questions about the source of its profits. The use of merger accounting by Dee has enabled it to include profits for a full year in respect of two of its most recent major acquisitions, both of which were acquired two-thirds of the way through its financial year.'

Booker was referring to the £21.8 million acquisition of Wellworth made on the 23rd December 1983 for which Dee included a full year's profits in its period to 28th April 1984, and to the £180.2 million purchase of International Stores on 28th December 1984 when profits for a full year were included in Dee's financial year ended on 27th April 1985. Although the justification for using merger accounting was not being questioned by Booker, of more concern was Dee's failure to adjust prior year comparatives to reflect the chosen approach.

Booker's defence document continued: 'But Dee disregards the generally accepted accounting practice in merger accounting of restating the results of the prior accounting year to include the results of the new company which would permit a proper comparison to be made one year with another. If the merger accounted profits from Wellworth and International Stores were restated in accordance with generally accepted accounting practice we estimate that Dee's rate of profit increase as reported would be reduced by two-thirds in the 1984/85 year and by one-third in the 1983/84 year.'

Assuming that Booker's estimates were correct the accounting policy results in a quite substantial difference between the profits as reported and those which would have resulted from a more traditional approach. Dee's justification for failing to adjust the comparatives was that there was no ruling accounting standard at the time. Now that the mergers and acquisitions standard has been published this loophole has been abolished once and for all.

The Dee/Booker episode highlights some of the motives and problems which underpin merger accounting. But what of those companies which are, for whatever reason, unable to adopt the principles and thereby find themselves with an element of goodwill which has to be written off? This may be a legacy of past acquisitions or perhaps a rare example of the accounting standard actually having its desired effect. Either way, this goodwill has to be written off thus opening the way for some further examples of accounting creativity.

The scope is somewhat limited since the goodwill has to be written off. The only question is over how it should be done? The options are either to make an immediate write-off to reserves or gradually to erode the goodwill through an annual charge to the profit and loss account. Although the accounting standard dealing with goodwill prefers immediate write-off, there is no compulsion to adopt this approach and therefore the decision will rest entirely with the company.

That decision will depend on the particular circumstances of the business. Most companies will, by and large, want to remove the goodwill from their balance sheets once and for all. Although this could result in a substantial one-off diminution of reserves, it is probably preferable to incurring a charge to profits over a period of time. Few businesses have enough confidence or indeed the foresight to predict what profits will be in the long term. Better then to take the write-off on the chin and below the line as soon as possible.

However, some companies, particularly those which have been highly acquisitive and built up large amounts of goodwill or firms such as advertising agencies where, as people businesses, the intangible asset features prominently, may find that they have insufficient reserves against which to make the write-off. It is something of an embarrassing problem, but it is not one which is insuperable. The accounting standard dealing with goodwill is generously flexible in setting the rules for establishing what is the 'economic life' of the goodwill over which it must be amortised.

The standard does go a little further than company law which makes no attempt whatsoever to define 'economic life', but not much. The standard does not specify either a maximum or minimum period for goodwill's 'economic life', saying only that it is the period over which benefits may reasonably be expected to accrue. That period has exactly the same length as a piece of string. A company can, therefore, take whatever period it likes. Only token regard need be afforded to the standard's appendix which sets out some of the factors which may be considered when assessing 'economic life'. These include such things as expected changes in markets or products; the expected future service period of key employees; and expected future demand, competition or other economic factors. Relevant though these factors may well be, companies may suddenly discover that they have an irrepressible desire to ignore them completely and employ a more pragmatic approach.

That pragmatic approach will not be unrelated to the

company's projected profits profile. The longer the 'economic life', the smaller will be the annual charge to the profit and loss account. This is the reason why some advertising agencies have decided to write their goodwill off over a period of 40 years. It is easy to see why that particular period was chosen but it is a little harder to justify it. Goodwill in advertising agencies tends to be closely linked to the abilities of the individuals who are normally the biggest and most important assets to the business. It does, therefore, seem bold to assume that these individuals will still be going strong and generating goodwill in 40 years' time. Contrary to popular belief, advertising folk are mortal.

The approach taken on goodwill can have quite an impact on a company's reported profit depending on whether it is written off immediately or over a period of time and, if so, what period. Take the situation where three similar companies each have goodwill of £40 million. Company A writes it off immediately and directly to reserves. Company B opts for amortisation over a period of four years. Company C takes the same approach but decides that the goodwill has an economic life of 40 years. The impact is as follows.

	Company A	Company B	Company C
	£m	£m	£m
Profits before goodwill	30	30	30
Goodwill written off	—	10	1
Profits before tax	30	20	29

It can be seen that, in profit and loss account terms there is an incentive to keep the charge for goodwill amortisation to a minimum. Goodwill can be something of an embarrassment as United Newspapers discovered during its 1985 battle to take over Fleet Holdings. The take-over was successful but on the way to winning its victory United had to fend off some rather tricky questions about what it was going to do with the £77.7 million which it had accumulated over the years, and which represented the large majority of the company's £100.8 million share capital and reserves. Fleet rightly pointed out that the goodwill would have to be written off, and argued that United had insufficient reserves which would therefore result in an annual charge to the profit and loss account of £3.9 million, if it was amortised over a period of 20 years. The question was clearly not of sufficient importance to preserve Fleet's independence, even though the response of United's financial advisers to the challenge was less than convincing. They argued that Fleet did have sufficient reserves for immediate write-off in the shape of the share premium account. That argument caused eyebrows to be raised in some accounting circles, and also highlights an area of some confusion. No one, it seems, is too sure about which reserves are available for the immediate write-off of goodwill. It is in such grey areas where the creative accountant thrives.

It is not just the share premium account about which there is doubt as to its suitability as a safe refuge for goodwill write-offs. It is also far from clear whether certain revaluation reserves can be used for such write-offs. Given the clear profit and loss incentives for companies to lose their goodwill as soon as possible there is a distinct temptation to take a rather liberal view on the interpretation on the complex company legislation governing the uses to which the share premium account and revaluation reserve can be put.

According to Company law an amount may only be transferred from the revaluation reserve to the profit and loss account where the amount in question was previously charged to the account or if it represents realised profits. In some cases, then, it may be inappropriate for a company to use its revaluation reserves for the goodwill write-off. However, the position is far from clear, which only encourages a company to take the view which is most sympathetic to its own cause.

The restrictions on the use of the share premium account are even more rigorous. Application may have to be made to the courts in certain circumstances where a company wants to tamper with its share premium account. Again, though, the issue is clouded with uncertainty. Legal opinions being what they are, however, it always seems possible to come up with a view which supports that of the company, and therefore goodwill write-offs against the share premium account will grow in popularity.

Where there is goodwill, there is a way to get rid of it without too much inconvenience, it seems. Now that there is a formal rule which insists on goodwill being written off, the focus of creative accounting attention will switch more clearly to the ways of avoiding and minimising its creation. As an accounting concept, goodwill must now be placed well and truly on the endangered species list. It is perhaps the best place for such an unwieldy animal.

One way of minimising its creation is simply to pretend that it doesn't exist. In other words, any goodwill which does arise is classified as something completely different. This approach is used most frequently in the publishing industry, where newspaper and magazine titles are attributed with a value. Clearly such titles are intangible assets, but by arguing that the overall value of the portfolio does not actually diminish, companies can avoid any amortisation charge.

It could be argued that when a publishing house buys a new title, the excess of the purchase price over net assets should be classified as goodwill, and therefore written off. However, such an approach is rarely taken, and the argument that the title retains a continuing value prevails. The purchase price is therefore capitalised, and, assuming that there is no impairment of the value of the complete portfolio of titles, then no depreciation is charged.

Although the publishing industry is that which is most suited to such a tactic, there are signs that other industries are looking for ways round the goodwill problem through the classification route. The arrival on company balance sheets of a variety of other intangible assets which are anything but goodwill may not be far off, as businesses desperately seek to avoid creating this clumsy beast.

The very existence of something like goodwill in the accountancy profession's handbook has only given an incentive for companies to become more imaginative in their ways of dealing with its inconvenience. If a more realistic approach to the item had been devised at the outset, then perhaps the sleight of accounting hand which has been applied so effectively to countering the problem would have been a little more restrained.

9

HOW to FLATTER FIXED ASSETS

*T*he great thing about fixed assets is that their values are completely mobile. For many companies these assets are the backbone of the business, providing the foundation and framework which allows it to carry out its operations. Yet, despite their importance, the rules which govern the reported values of fixed assets are remarkably flexible.

That flexibility is the more remarkable given the starting-point for the valuation process. This will, in the large majority of cases, be the cost of the asset which is rarely open to manipulation. Be it a company car or chunk of land, the purchase price will set the benchmark from which the creative accounting process begins. There is little scope for tampering with original cost but after that there is unlimited scope for making fixed assets work for the business in every sense of the phrase. That scope is more pronounced because the value placed on the assets can be adjusted either upwards or downwards almost at will.

The justification for this creativity is actually embodied in company law, which permits three different bases for valuations of fixed assets to be adopted. Alongside the old favourite of historical cost, which is simply the price paid for an asset, the legislation also allows market valuations to be used. Companies can also state their fixed assets at current cost, although the law gives no indication of what it means by this rather vague term. Given this overt approval of a variety of valuation methods it is not surprising that most businesses are more than happy to take advantage of them.

This array of choices is offered in recognition of the corporate sector's desire to reflect more fairly the value of its assets to the respective businesses. It is not an unreasonable proposition. However, the decision on what basis or combination of bases to use rests solely with the company, thereby opening the way for a large amount of creativity which becomes inevitable when subjective judgments are called for in large quantities.

That subjectivity, and the dilemmas it can cause, is illustrated by the approach that British Airways has taken on its fleet of Concordes. Supersonic and sleek the jet may be, but it is valued at nothing in the airline's accounts. The decision to write the fleet down to nil value was implemented some time ago. The other options for British Airways would be to put the Concorde fleet in the accounts at cost less depreciation, which would put the value in the high millions: to use current cost, that is the amount that would be needed to replace the fleet at today's prices which would run into billions. Three vastly differing values for exactly the same aeroplane.

British Airways has something of a reputation for playing around with the asset lives of its other aircraft and a review of their accounts over a period of time illustrates this. In 1979/80, for instance, it extended the operational lives of its Boeing 747 and Tristar fleets from 14 to 16 years. In the same year helicopter lives were standardised at 14 years. The effect of these changes was to reduce the British Airways Board's depreciation charge by £7.6 million, which is quite significant in terms of its overall loss before tax of £4.9 million. In 1981/82 the economic lives and residual values Tristar fleet was written down along with other aircraft to amounts 'estimated to be recoverable during their remaining lives'. By 1984/85, British Airways had reduced further specific information on asset lives saying only that 'operational lives and residual values are reviewed annually in the light of experience and changing circumstances'.

The approach which is adopted for fixed asset valuations can clearly have quite an impact on a company's accounts. The choice is therefore not taken lightly, and will depend as much on the company's own requirements as it will on the over-riding obligation to show a true and fair view of the business. It is also quite complex because not only must a decision be taken on the valuation basis but also on the consequent rates of depreciation which must be charged.

The advantages of beefing up the balance sheet through an upward fixed asset revaluation must be weighed against the increased depreciation which will accrue and which must be charged each year to the profit and loss account. A careful juggling of valuation and depreciation will usually allow a company to arrive at a combination which will maximise the impact on the balance sheet and minimise its effect on the profit and loss account.

So far the term 'fixed assets' has been used fairly loosely. It would be wrong, however, to assume that all the assets which fall into this category are suitable targets for manipulation in both directions. Certainly depreciation rates can be used to influence in a downward direction the stated value of all fixed assets, but upward revaluations can only be applied to certain types. In the main it is land and buildings which are the most appropriate candidates for revaluations. Anybody who has got involved in either buying or selling a house will be well aware that property prices are apparently unaware of the laws of gravity, and it is hardly surprising that some companies want to show how this boom has affected their own land and buildings.

The wish to reflect increasing property prices is under-standable. However, the question of identifying and quantify-ing those increases in order to reflect them in the accounts is another matter. Again, those who have had any involvement with the property market will know that the valuations which are attributed to a property can vary quite considerably.

The number of different valuations equates exactly with the number of estate agents who are asked to pass an opinion. As house sellers are acutely aware, there is only one real valuation, and that is the price at which a buyer is prepared to part with his hard-earned cash. The exact value is therefore easy to determine when a sale takes place, but it is not difficult to see that there is room for considerable flexibility when the valuation of a company's assets is carried out purely for academic accounting purposes.

So broad are the valuation bands in the real world that there is no need for a company to retreat to fantasy land in order to come up with a figure for its land and buildings which meets its needs. It would be wrong to suggest that the surveying profession is failing in its duties to provide fair and independent advice. Rather it is the vagaries of the property market which allows such differing valuations. That said, there have been cases where a company has had a property revaluation carried out by one firm of surveyors, and, when this has failed to produce the anticipated results, another revaluation has been immediately summoned from a different firm so that more appropriate values can be established. Such extreme cases are the exception rather than the rule, but while one surveyor's opinion continues to be as good as the next surveyor's opinion, there is always going to be a lot of room for manoeuvre.

However, although property is the most obvious candidate for revaluation, it does not have exclusive rights. Other fixed assets can also be the target for a rethink. The rationale for the revaluation of plant and machinery comes from the accountancy profession's fixation with inflation accounting. So far it has failed miserably to introduce an acceptable and appropriate method of dealing with the effect of changing prices on a company's accounts. However, in the process of failure, it has encouraged businesses to look more carefully at what their assets are worth. One of the major features of inflation accounting is its preoccupation with the current cost of assets, in other words what they would cost to replace. In times of rising prices this implies rising replacement costs and hence rising valuations, not just of property but also of the plant and machinery which is so important, particularly for manufacturing companies.

Although the business community has comprehensively rejected the efforts made by the accountancy profession to introduce a full-scale system of inflation accounting, it has not been averse to plucking out the elements of such a system which work to its benefit. What we have seen, then, is some companies taking advantage of the positive points but ignoring the countering negative points, by adopting a very one-sided version of inflation accounting. In essence this has been achieved through the revaluation of fixed assets. Many companies are now using this shorthand version of inflation accounting by applying indices to their fixed assets, in order to enhance and strengthen their balance-sheets.

The BOC Group is one such company which employs this approach, adopting what it quaintly calls the 'modified historical cost accounting convention'. Under this convention the gross book value of most of the group's fixed assets is recorded at current replacement cost or the economic value of those assets if this is lower. To be fair to BOC it has, in the past, also given equal prominence to fully-fledged current cost accounts, but such levels of disclosure tend to be the exception rather than the rule.

Such an approach is less sinister if it is applied consistently year on year, and if it is applied universally throughout the group. More worrying are those companies which are a little more selective about their treatment of fixed assets. By picking and choosing which assets are to be revalued and when this is to be done a company retains much greater control over the figures it reports.

For some companies, the policies on fixed asset valuation seem to owe more to the rules of stud poker than to accounting conventions. The name of the game is to give away enough to maintain interest but never so much that people will know exactly what you have. As with all card games there will always be those who do not play by the rules. Fixed asset revaluations are, therefore, something akin to the ace up the sleeve which can be produced when the game is not going your way. That ace will be played only as an act of last resort, which is why it is not unusual to see fixed asset revaluations featuring prominently as part of a defence against an unwanted take-over.

It is a fairly standard tactic, these days, for a company which is on the wrong end of a hostile bid miraculously to come up with a new revaluation for its fixed assets which demonstrates quite conclusively that the predator has grossly underestimated the value of the business and is merely attempting to pick it up on the cheap. So common is the tactic that its impact is often undermined. However, there is no doubt that asset valuations still remain as one of the most contentious areas of debate during take-over battles.

Be it as part of bid defence or an attempt to beef up the balance sheet, or a genuine effort to reflect true value to the business, fixed asset valuations will always present opportunities for creative accounting. These opportunities are not restricted to the balance sheet since the consequent charge to the profit and loss account for depreciation will also be affected.

Take three companies, A, B and C, which all buy identical fixed assets for £20,000 on 1 January 1986. The estimated life of this type of asset is 10 years after which it will have no residual value. Company A carries out no revaluations of the asset but on 31 December 1988 both B and C decide that it is then worth £28,000. On 31 December 1990, Company C carries out a further revaluation of the asset and estimates that on that date it is worth £30,000. A year later on 31 December 1991 all three companies sell their assets for an identical price of £30,000. The transactions will be recorded in the books of A, B and C as follows on page 98.

The differing approaches to valuations of the assets also affects the total charge made to the profit and loss account over the period. The total effect is summarised on page 98.

The illustration assumes that the surpluses on the revaluations carried out by Companies B and C are incorporated in the balance sheet through a revaluation reserve. Similarly, an element of the surplus on disposal will be dealt with through the same reserve as it switches from being 'unrealised' to 'realised'. It also assumes that asset disposals are treated as part of profits for the year rather than being disclosed separately or below the line as an extraordinary item.

It is apparent that the differing valuation approaches result in widely differing impacts on the profit and loss account. Although Company A receives no benefit to its balance sheet

	Company A	Company B	Company C
	£'000	£'000	£'000
Cost 1.1.86	20	20	20
Depreciation to 31.12.88	(6)	(6)	(6)
	14	14	14
Revaluation 31.12.88	—	14	14
Net Book Value 31.12.88	14	28	28
Depreciation to 31.12.90	(4)	(8)	(8)
	10	20	20
Revaluation 31.12.90	—	—	10
Net Book Value 31.12.90	10	20	30
Depreciation to 31.12.91	(2)	(4)	(6)
Net Book Value 31.12.91	8	16	24
Sales Proceeds	30	30	30
Net Book Value 31.12.91	(8)	(16)	(24)
Surplus on Disposal	22	14	6

	Company A	Company B	Company C
	£'000	£'000	£'000
Surplus on Disposal	22	14	6
Total Depreciation Charged	(12)	(18)	(20)
Net Effect	10	(4)	(14)

by retaining the asset at cost throughout the period, it actually increases its profit by £10,000. Both Companies B and C, however, show reductions in their reported profits. It therefore appears that there is a strong incentive for a business not to incorporate asset revaluations. Certainly, the balance sheet does not benefit but reported profits will appear that much better. Also, if a company is judged on the basis of the return that it makes on assets, there is a clear advantage in sticking with historical cost, since the business will be reporting higher profits on lower asset values. Such management and performance accounting can be dangerous, however, since it is liable to distort the real level of achievement.

The inequality of the differing approaches has not been lost on the creative accountant. Rather than suffer from a reduction in reported profits, many companies overcome the problem by including their realised revaluation surplus as part of the profit on disposal of the asset.

The illustration below shows how this approach serves to equalise the net effect on reported profits for the period that the asset is held:

	Company A	Company B	Company C
£'000	£'000	£'000	£'000
Surplus on Disposal	22	14	6
Realised Revaluation Surplus	—	14	24
Depreciation Charged	(12)	(18)	(24)
Net Effect	10	10	10

By adopting this approach both Companies B and C catch up with Company A in the year of disposal. In doing so, however, they will alter the level of profit which is reported at the time of the sale, since they will also include an element of the realised revaluation surplus. This reflects the different amounts of depreciation which have been charged as a result of the changes in the value attributed to the asset. The profit reported on the disposals will therefore be:

	Company A	Company B	Company C
	£'000	£'000	£'000
Surplus on Disposal	22	14	6
Realised Revaluation Surplus	—	14	24
Reported Profit on Disposal	22	28	30

Although the net effect on all three companies is exactly the same over the period, the timing of the reporting of the profits differs. The policy that a business adopts is likely to be influenced, then, by the profits profile which is most appropriate to its particular needs.

That profits profile is quite critical. A company which has had a particularly good financial year, and which has been revaluing some of its assets, may not need to take account of the element of profit which is contained in the revaluation reserve. It may be quite happy just to take account of the surplus which arises when deducting from the sales proceeds the net book value at the date of disposal. The additional profit is in effect dealt with directly through reserves and need not enter the profit and loss account at all. There are moves afoot at the ASC to try and discourage this approach. Even so, companies will still be able to maintain substantial control over the profits they actually report. By insisting that the realisation of a revaluation reserve is dealt with in the profit and loss account, it is almost an encouragement for companies to manipulate their reported profits by careful timing of asset disposals.

One way to reduce the amount of profit that has to be dealt with through the revaluation reserve is actually to credit less to it in the first place. It may sound easier said than done and it also has the hallmarks of something with which the standard setters may not be too enamoured, but it can be argued that company legislation allows just such an approach. The key to this example of creative accounting is the treatment of the accumulated depreciation which has already been charged to the profit and loss account before a revaluation is carried out. The traditional approach is to credit that accumulated depreciation to the revaluation reserve, but it does appear that it is possible simply to write it back to the profit and loss account in the year of the revaluation.

Take an asset which cost £2 million with a life of ten years and with no residual value. Half-way through its life the company decides to revalue it to £3 million. At the date of and immediately before the revaluation the asset will have a net book value of £1 million (the cost of £2 million less five years' depreciation at £200,000 a year). On revaluation, under traditional accounting practices, the asset's net book value immediately becomes £3 million and at the same time an amount of £2 million is credited to the revaluation reserve (the revalued amount of £3 million less the previous net book value of £1 million). Included in that credit to the revaluation reserve is an accumulated depreciation of £1 million which will stay there until such time as the asset is sold.

However, the alternative to this traditional approach is actually to write back the accumulated depreciation to the profit and loss account, thus transferring to the revaluation reserve only the difference between the revalued amount and the original cost of the asset. Under this method the net book value of the asset immediately after the revaluation will still be £3 million. However, the transfer to the revaluation reserve will be restricted to £1 million (the revalued amount of £3 million less the original cost of the asset of £2 million). The difference of £1 million is the accumulated depreciation which had been charged to the profit and loss account in the five years before the revaluation. That £1 million is then credited to the profit and loss account providing a much welcomed boost to profits. It is a useful trick and it is not surprising that the ASC is trying very hard to outlaw it.

It is a particularly useful approach for companies which are facing a take-over. Not only does an asset revaluation lend a helping hand to the balance sheet, at the same time it also increases reported profits at a time when a company is quite desperate to present its performance and prospects in the most beneficial light. The method also has advantages for a business which is not in the awkward position of having to ward off an unwanted bid. In these cases it allows a company to take credit for the revaluation surplus much earlier than would otherwise be possible. This may give rise to questions over whether or not the credited accumulated depreciation constitutes realised profits but these will not always be critical. In effect a company is indulging in a little profits smoothing. So, rather than have a big profit in the year of disposal, a business will simply take credit for it on a more gradual basis.

The main advantage is to bring forward the year in which the profit is recognised, which can be very useful particularly if there are no immediate plans to sell the asset. However, the method also helps to do away with unwelcome peaks in the profit profile. One of the keys to a successful working relationship with the stock market is for a company to demonstrate that it has a steady and upward profits trend. The stock market does not like unusual one-off factors. If a company was therefore to take all its profits on asset sales in the year of disposal, this may well result in a large lump which the stock market may immediately dismiss as being an unusual, non-recurring factor. Worse still, those profits might be deemed to be extraordinary and left out of the equation altogether.

As a variation on the theme of profits smoothing, company law also appears to permit a company to adopt a method of split depreciation. This approach is also under attack from the ASC and may subsequently be outlawed. The approach was adopted by Woolworth in its 1984 accounts but dropped a year later. Split depreciation allows a company to revalue its assets and base its depreciation charge not on the new revalued amount but on the old historical cost amount. The effect is quite stunning since the balance-sheet benefits from the increased value of the assets, but the profit and loss account incurs a much smaller depreciation charge. The difference between the charge on the revalued basis and the charge on the historical basis is taken direct to the revaluation reserve. Although the method aroused some criticism when first employed, and subsequently incurred the wrath of the ASC, it actually removes some of the distortions of reported profits which can arise when an asset is finally sold. This factor is, it seems, not of a sufficiently redeeming nature for a wider use of split depreciation to be encouraged and it is now effectively outlawed.

So far, the creative accounting aspects of dealing with fixed assets have concentrated very much on revaluing assets upward. However, there is also some scope for manipulating reported results by reducing the value at which assets are carried. It may not seem to be a particularly sensible thing to do; after all, there does not seem much merit in deliberately understating what a business is worth. This might only encourage a takeover bid, or, for quoted companies, result in some weakness in the share price.

That may well be so but as a short term tactical measure, the writing down of fixed assets can be quite useful. It is perhaps most appropriate for businesses which have recently suffered from a difficult trading time. This may have been due to specific difficulties within an industry, more general economic problems as witnessed in the recent recession, or simply because of bad and inefficient management. For these companies the main objective may simply be one of survival. The general downturn in the trading performance will probably have been accompanied by a large element of dissatisfaction either from shareholders, the company's bankers, or indeed both. They will want to see change, and to help them get it they may insist on a new team of management which is charged with the specific responsibility of restoring the company's fortunes. The risks for such a team are high. Failure to accomplish the task may result in a loss of credibility, which may restrict the opportunities for future gainful employment. At the same time the rewards are equally attractive. The increasing use of share option schemes for these crisis and rescue management teams can mean that they have the chance to become very wealthy if they do knock a business back into shape. It is the size of those rewards and the cost of failure which create a climate which encourages creative accounting.

It is a climate in which there are considerable benefits from starting out with a low asset base and gradually building up. The smaller the level of assets at the start, the more pronounced subsequent increases will be. Similarly the lower the profits at the beginning, the easier it will be to improve on them.

Imagine a company which, through no fault of the management, has produced some poor trading figures: business has simply been bad. However, the company's bankers blame the management and threaten to withdraw credit facilities if there isn't a change at the top. Reluctantly the non-executive directors bow to this threat of imminent liquidation and replace the senior management team with some fresh blood. The change-over takes place just after the year end although there had been sufficient time for the old management to draw up draft accounts. The company has fixed assets with a book value of £100 million and depreciation is charged at the rate of 10 per cent a year. The business is making profits after all charges, but before tax and depreciation, of £15 million. The new team takes over and on examining the business decides that the fixed assets are worth only half the amount at which they are stated in the accounts. They immediately decide, therefore, on a substantial write-down in asset values which, because of its nature, will be treated as an extraordinary item and therefore disclosed below the line which excludes it from pre-tax profits calculations and the important earnings per share calculations. The accounts of the old and new management would be published as follows:

	Old £m	New £m
Trading Profit	15	15
Depreciation	(10)	(5)
Pre-Tax Profit	5	10
Extraordinary Item	—	(50)
Net Fixed Asset Value	90	45

The impact of the accounting changes brought about by the new management are swift and sudden. At a stroke the company doubles its pre-tax profits. Although the asset value attributable to the business is halved, the reported return earned on those fixed assets is increased from 5.6 per cent under the old management to 22.2 per cent under the new team. It is a huge difference and gives the immediate impression that the new management has got the business under control and is steering it along the road to recovery. That impression is of course misleading. The old management could have obtained exactly the same result by adopting a similar accounting policy.

To the outside world it appears, however, as if the new management is at last making the assets sweat. The only sweating in fact is done by the creative accountants as they pore over the books in search of other ways to portray the new management in a more favourable light and at the same time make the financial performance under the old management look as bleak as possible.

It is a common occurrence nowadays for new management teams to make substantial provisions and write-downs in the year of their arrival in an effort to get all the bad news out of the way at one fell swoop. That bad news can be blamed on the ineptitude of their predecessors, so, although the company may report an horrendous set of figures, the new management are free from any responsibility for the catastrophe. More important, from their point of view, the path has been cleared for the company to be rationalised and restructured, if such things are needed, without incurring unfortunate blots on the financial performance by which they will be judged.

It must also be remembered that having written the assets down, the new management is not committed to maintaining them in the books at that level. The right to revalue those same assets in an upward direction is not foregone. When the time is right the values could be reinstated with all the benefits which were explored earlier. As time passes, the new management would be able to restore the asset base which it had so deliberately eroded when it first took office. This is not to say that the improvement in the business is purely artificial and simply the work of slick accounting practices. For the new team to prove its real worth, it will have to wring out some genuine improvements in the company's operations. However, what this creative accounting does is to exaggerate the extent of that improvement and contrast much more starkly the performance between old and new.

Such massive depreciation write-downs against fixed assets tend to be limited to the type of situations envisaged above. However, there may well be instances when a company wants to accelerate the depreciation it charges. The rate which is chosen is purely abitrary, as is the method which is adopted, so the opportunities for dabbling with depreciation are legion. Indeed it is very difficult for a company's auditors to argue with the basis which is ultimately adopted, since the depreciation charge is little more than a stab in the dark at assessing the natural wear and tear which any asset incurs. Take the company car for instance. It may be depreciated equally over 4 years at 25 per cent a year. Yet as all new car owners know, the biggest slab of depreciation is incurred the minute the new vehicle is driven proudly off the garage forecourt.

Given, therefore, that the depreciation charge can never be more than a rough approximation of the decline in an asset's value it is quite simple for a company to make gentle adjustments to the amount which is actually charged either by reviewing asset lives, altering assumptions on residual values, or adjusting the actual rate applied. Although changes in residual values might technically be regarded as errors of original estimation, and the financial effect treated as a prior-year adjustment, there is an increasing tendency to deal with any consequent over depreciation as a reduction to the current year's charge or as write-back to profits. Either way, profits are boosted.

There is no need to resort to the blatant creativity indulged in by some of the nationalised industries in the 1970s. Faced with the embarrassing prospect of earning outrageously healthy profits, both the Electricity and Gas industries came up with the wonderful idea of charging something known as 'supplementary depreciation'. There was of course nothing illegal about this and the charge was made with the blessing of the auditors. The justification for the charge came from a variation on the theme of current cost accounting, but to the cynics it looked like a very clever piece of creative accounting.

Companies in the private sector are a little more subtle, and careful planning of the depreciation charge can allow a business to take advantage of the years of plenty, by increasing the amount which is reported, in order to have something in reserve for the years of famine. Once again it is simply a question of smoothing the profits.

Perhaps the only limiting factor on the amount of

depreciation which can be charged is the level of the fixed assets against which to charge it. The classification of what assets are deemed to be fixed is, therefore, highly significant, and, as is often the case, there are sufficient areas which are suitably grey in colour to allow a company some flexibility.

The argument is essentially that of what is capital and what is revenue expenditure? This is a question of particular interest to the Inland Revenue since the answer can have a bearing on a company's tax liability. The general rule is that fixed assets are those which the company intends to use on a continuing basis. This is clear enough but there are a number of areas where the basic rule is open to interpretation.

For instance, although company law does not allow businesses to capitalise research costs, in special circumstances it does permit the capitalisation of development costs. But where does research stop and development begin? The line between the two is thin and not clearly drawn, and even when the division is established, the amount which can be capitalised is still open to debate. The kind of costs which could be capitalised include staff costs, material costs, overheads and even depreciation itself. Clearly the more a company can classify as development expenditure the less it will have to charge against profits for the year. Not only is the charge to profits reduced, but also deferred, since the development costs as capitalised need not be amortised until such time as the programme moves into commercial production. Once again a company is presented with an excellent opportunity to control its flow of profits. The amount of development expenditure actually charged will rely to a large extent on the company's internal cost allocation structure and, within reason, it should be possible to turn the flow on and off in order to influence the reported profits in any particular year.

A second grey area is that relating to the treatment of computer software which has become an important aspect of almost all commercial life. In the early days the tendency was to write such costs off straight to the profit and loss account when they were incurred. However, as these costs grew both in frequency and in magnitude, there has been a similar increase in the number of companies looking to mitigate the impact by treating the expenditure as being capital in nature. Arguments can be presented for treating computer software as either fixed or intangible assets depending on how it was acquired or developed. Again the company can exercise some control over these costs, with the decision being based more on its own needs than on the rather vague criteria which must be examined in reaching that decision.

A further item which is growing in popularity as a source of capitalisation is the interest which is incurred on borrowings raised to finance the construction of a fixed asset. The BOC Group has adopted this approach for some time, and now the food retailing sector, with its huge expenditure on store development programmes, is following suit. Both Tesco and J Sainsbury capitalise interest on store development which gives them a seemingly unfair profits advantage over those chains which can afford to finance stores development out of internally generated cash funds. More of this, though, in the chapter dealing with cash and borrowings.

In certain circumstances it might even be possible to avoid charging any depreciation at all. For instance, some breweries and retailers argue that their pubs and shops should not be depreciated because they are constantly being upgraded and refurbished, so that they are maintained as if they were new. It may appear to be illegal, but this is not the case, and the accounting profession is curiously silent on the issue. However, although maintenance expenditure is clearly a major part of such a company's costs, it is a discretionary charge. Therefore, in the years of plenty it can be accelerated, and in the lean years reduced. That is a luxury which is not readily available under the standard depreciation rules.

Similarly certain shipping companies, which were hit by the recession in the industry, and forced to lay up vessels, simply decided to abandon any depreciation charge. The argument was that while the asset was not being used then there was no need to depreciate it, which conveniently overlooked the fact that the value of those vessels had actually tumbled quite dramatically as a result of the overcapacity in the industry. If anything, more depreciation was called for rather than less.

The flexibility already outlined may seem enough to keep most creative accountants happy, but there is a bonus in the shape of the treatments which are available for dealing with the government grants given for specific fixed assets. Two options are offered. Either the asset's cost is reduced by the amount of the grant, or it may be treated as a deferred credit with a proportion transferred annually to revenue. The choice will again affect the reported figures, and will be tailored to meet the company's own requirements.

Fixed assets then are pliable, flexible and mobile. Everything then except fixed!

10

HOW to CULTIVATE CURRENT ASSETS and LIABILITIES

A company's debtors and creditors tend to be rather overshadowed by their more illustrious neighbours of stock and cash or borrowings in the current assets area of the balance-sheet. The lack of attention which is paid to them is misplaced if not misguided, since debtor and creditor management can be an important influence in determining a company's cash flow position. It follows that the quicker that debts are collected and the slower that creditors are paid, the better. This frees funds which would otherwise have been financing working capital requirements for use elsewhere in the business. However, moderation, as with all things, is called for. An over-zealous approach to working capital management could, if not carefully controlled, result in a disproportionate amount of current liability arising. If the company's resources are tied up in long term and fixed assets, then it may face problems in meeting the short term liabilities as they fall due.

A careful analysis, then, of the relationship between creditors and debtors can give an important indication of the company's performance and prospects. A fairly even match between the two is normally quite acceptable although this must also be set against the level of the company's other current assets. Similarly, an examination of the relationship between the debtors and creditors and the sales and purchases which gave rise to them can be equally informative. If turn over is falling then the level of debtors would be expected to follow suit, and a failure for it to do so might be an indication of some kind of problem with the collection procedures.

Although a detailed examination of debtors and creditors is perhaps not a regular feature of the City's assessment of a company's performance and prospects, this does not mean that these current assets and liabilities can be left to their own devices. Once again any unusual fluctuations in the figures will be picked up and used as evidence against the company, so it is still important to ensure that the relevant figures proceed in a quiet and orderly fashion. The converse of this is that both debtors and creditors can be used in a positive fashion to help achieve this objective.

The most obvious area for attention is the ominous sounding subject of bad debts. As a rule these are things to be avoided. Careful credit control and vetting of new customers can help mitigate the circumstances where bad debts might arise, but it is a sad fact of commercial life that some businesses simply cannot pay their way and go to the wall leaving their creditors high and dry, and facing an unwelcome bad debt provision.

It therefore becomes important for a company to take a realistic attitude to the problem and plan ahead for the inevitable debts which will occur. That planning comes in the shape of providing for bad debts in the most constructive fashion. Often the best approach will be to make a general provision on an annual basis. This is not dissimilar to the concept of making an annual provision for obsolescent stock. Again it has the advantage of bringing an element of consistency to the situation, which will offset the discomfort of the charge which has to be made to the profit and loss account.

The general bad debt provision may simply be calculated as a consistent proportion of the total debtors. On the other hand, it may be linked to the age of debtors. The longer the debt has been outstanding the less chance there is of it being recovered, and thus requiring a subsequent provision. The company may therefore provide against all debts over a certain age, and then make provisions against the younger debts on a reducing scale of proportions. A prudent approach to bad debt provisions at an early stage will reduce the chances of a company being taken by surprise later should a large debt suddenly go bad. Even if such a specific bad debt had not been provided against there might be no need to incur an ugly write-off scar, since this can be set against the general provision which had already been created. The provision will then require some topping up in subsequent years but this can be done in a more leisurely and less obtrusive fashion.

The same general provision can also be used as an accounting tool for assisting with the profits smoothing process. The provision is gradually built up while profits growth is good. When those increases slow down or even go into decline, the company will be able to reduce the impact of this change in fortunes either by halting any further additions to the bad debt provision, or, in some cases, actually by releasing a part of the provision and writing it back as a contributor to profit for the year on the grounds that it is no longer necessary. This affords a very useful element of control over the reported profits which is perhaps not in itself sufficient to combat any major change in fortunes, but can certainly help to remove some of the smaller unwanted fluctuations.

The opportunities for inflating debtors are somewhat limited, although a company can perhaps make some attempt to do so by its approach on trade discounts. These are normally offered as an incentive for debtors to pay their invoices promptly and will take the form of a reduction in the cash which is due on settlement. The sooner the customer pays the greater the discount. Normally a company will include the gross amount of the invoice value as part of sales for the year. Any discounts which are claimed will be treated as marketing or administrative costs, and charged as an expense rather than as a reduction of sales value. A company might therefore be tempted to adopt a similar approach to the year end debtors which will include the gross amounts outstanding. The problem with this is that it can then be argued that the debts are being stated at more than their net realisable value, which conflicts with company law. In this position the company will be forced to make some provision for those discounts. This, of course, is an arbitrary decision which will be only loosely based on the past take-up of discounts.

There might also be an added element of flexibility in the way that the provision for the discounts is disclosed. The company could well argue that it has the right to choose to report the provision in the accounts either as a reduction of total debtors or as an addition to its creditors. Normally the set-off between assets and liabilities is forbidden, but this does not affect the situation relating to discounts. In fact the company might well struggle to try and justify not setting the provision against debtors, since these would still be disclosed at an amount greater than their net realisable value. It is worth a try though.

One further way which might be considered as a means of pushing up the figure reported in the accounts as debtors, is to boost the level of prepayments. These relate to expenses which have been settled in one accounting period but which relate in part to a subsequent year. Telephone bills for instance, always charge the rental of the equipment one quarter in advance. Rates are also normally paid in advance, and, unless the rateable year coincides with the company's own accounting period, then there will be some element of prepayment. Any such amounts will be excluded from the charge to profits for the year and treated as an asset of the company. The prepayments can be disclosed either as a separate category in the balance-sheet or as part of debtors.

So if a company wants, for some reason, to boost its total debtors, perhaps to offset the impact of some unusually high bad debt provision, then it might well resort to prepayments as the means of accomplishing this. There are two difficulties with this. First the bringing forward of the payment will result in a reduction in cash, although this may actually be part of the strategy. The second problem is that it is often hard to find items which can be categorised as prepayments. There is a limit to the number of 'phone bills and rate demands which can be settled ahead of the year end. However, if the company leases some or all of its buildings, then it may be possible to make some substantial prepayment of rentals for the forthcoming year. However, the desire for creative accounting must be tempered by the commercial viability of the decision. If the prepayment is going to result in a reduction of income which might have been earned on the cash then it should not be made.

This artificial increase in debtors is only reflected in the main balance-sheet. The observant reader of the accounts will discover what the company has done if he refers to the notes to the accounts. The analysis of the total debtors figure which must be provided has to disclose as a separate item the amount of any prepayments. This disclosure requirement perhaps reduces the effectiveness of the tactic although the company can still gamble on shareholders and other interested parties failing to delve as deep as the notes to the accounts.

Scope for manipulation of a company's working capital is not, of course, restricted to debtors, and creditors have their fair share to contribute to the creative accountant's armoury. Given that creditors are almost the mirror image of debtors it will come as no surprise to discover that many of the techniques which can be used to improve the superficial impression of a set of accounts are the exact opposite of those which can be used when dealing with amounts which are owed by customers.

Take trade discounts for instance. While it is the company which is offering these to debtors there is an incentive to account for the gross amount of the invoice. However, once the boot is switched to the other foot, and it is the company itself which is in a position to claim discounts through prompt payment, then there will be a tendency to treat invoices from suppliers on a net basis after deducting the discount receivable. This has the immediate effect of reducing the cost of sales and at the same time reducing the amount which is disclosed in the balance sheet as trade creditors.

The same role reversal is encountered when dealing with the converse of prepayments which are known as accruals. The purpose of these is to take account of the cost of goods or services of which the company has had the benefit but for which it has not yet been invoiced. These may take the form of goods delivered towards the end of the year which the supplier has not got round to invoicing. Another example is that old faithful the telephone bill: for while the equipment rental is charged in advance, the actual calls made are billed in arrears. Thus a company is obliged to accrue for the cost of those calls which were made before the year end, but which had not been invoiced at that date.

Clearly there is an element of subjective judgment involved in assessing what levels of accruals ought to be made. Often that subjectivity is removed by the arrival of an invoice shortly after the year end and before the accounts are finalised. However, there will be times when the company has to use little more than guesswork when deciding what accruals to make. Assuming that the approach adopted is not outrageous, it should be possible for the managment to make some gentle understatement of the true amount. The effect of understating the accruals is to reduce the liability which has to be disclosed in the balance-sheet and, at the same time, to reduce the expenses which are charge to the profit and loss account in the year. It should be stressed that consistent material understatement of such liabilities is getting very close to the bone which is marked fraud. This of course is against the principle of creative accounting, which relies for its success and credibility on strict compliance with the law.

The line between creative accounting and fraud can sometimes be very thin and very frail. The line sometimes disappears from view altogether when the question of recognising liabilities is addressed. The basic rule which runs throughout the standards laid down by the accountancy profession, is that all losses should be recognised and provided for as soon as their existence is discovered, while profits should only be accounted for when they are realised. It is a rule, however, which is often broken. There is a distinct reluctance among companies to take account of some liabilities which are looming on the horizon. The uncertainty which often surrounds these items makes it easier for a company to dismiss them, particularly when the potential liability would not crystallise until some time in the future.

The legal action which the liquidator of Laker Airways brought against British Airways and other airlines over their alleged cooperation in bringing about Sir Freddie Laker's downfall, is a prime example of the repercussions of failing to recognise a liability. In the final analysis that legal action was to delay the privatisation of British Airways and involve it in a costly out of court settlement. Yet, for a long time, the world's favourite airline took no account of the potential cost to the company. The furthest it went was to disclose the existence of the action as a contingent liability in the notes to the accounts. All this did, however, was to draw the reader's attention to the lawsuit, and it did not affect the figures in the financial statements at all. One of the arguments used in defence of this approach was that to make a provision in the accounts could have prejudiced BA's defence of the action.

The same argument is put forward by other companies who face some kind of legal action. Whatever the nature or size of such lawsuits the policy always seems to be the same. The claims are ignored normally because the company's legal advisers have said that the claims are frivolous and have no substance in law. The problem is that this is exactly what legal advisers are for. The firm of solicitors which constantly tells its corporate clients: 'Sorry lads, they've got you bang to rights on this one', tends to find itself back on conveyancing fairly promptly. While the suggestion that to make a provision for the potential cost of the claims is as good as an admission of guilt may have some credence, it may not always be the best course of action.

Once the watching world, and in particular the City, is aware of the existence of any substantial legal actions, the uncertainty may well be reflected immediately in the share price. If this is the case, then the company may have little to lose by making a quiet provision in the accounts. Should the case ultimately go against it, then at least the costs involved will have already been taken account of and the reported results and the share price will not suffer again. On the other hand, if the company wins the case then the provision can be written back to profits at a later date at the company's convenience. The decision on whether or not to provide will not just be governed by the legal considerations but also by the company's own financial performance. If, in the year when the legal claims first come to light, the company's profits are under pressure, then it may be better to defer any provision until the next accounting period when things might have picked up.

Of course, legal actions are not the only type of liability which may arise. However, the principles of recognition are very similar, although less constrained, since the legal implications will not feature as largely in the equation. The underlying considerations, though, are essentially unchanged and the decision on the provision will be dependent on the company's current trading and projected profits profile.

It would be misleading to suggest that liabilities are just nasty things which have to be avoided wherever possible. There are positive creative accounting points which should not be overlooked. These are exactly the same as those which apply to the assessment of bad debt provisions. By setting up a liability, perhaps for warranty agreements on the company's products, the business is able to maintain stability within the reported results and avoid any nasty shocks to the system which could threaten to ruin the smoothing process.

The management should not overlook either the benefits of the taking it on the chin approach to liabilities and provisions. This is discussed in more detail in the chapter on extraordinary items. In summary, though, it allows a company to take all the bad news in one year to get it out of the way once and for all. This may involve heavy write-offs and provisions which will often be disclosed below the line and thus ignored from the profits and earnings calculations. Once these provisions are set up, they are then carried forward in the balance-sheet and the actual costs are written off to them as and when they are incurred, thus leaving the company's trading performance unscathed.

There is some uncertainty and confusion over how such provisions should be disclosed in the accounts. It is clearly in the company's interests to give as little away as possible about them, if they are being used as part of the smoothing process, or if they relate to some contended legal action. However, the Companies Acts have anticipated these liabilities, and there is a requirement for 'provisions for liabilities and charges' to be disclosed as a separate item in the balance-sheet with a more detailed analysis being presented by way of a note to the accounts. The 1985 Act also goes as far as providing a definition of these items describing them as: 'Any amount retained as reasonably necessary for the purpose of providing for any liability or loss which is either likely to be incurred or certain to be incurred but uncertain as to the amount or as to the date on which it will arise.'

The law seems to be quite precise on this point and it will be difficult to argue that these provisions should be disclosed as part of the trade creditors figure or as an accrual. There may be some cases where such arguments can be presented and accepted, and it will always be worth making an effort to press for the less explicit disclosure. However, if the company's auditors insist on the provisions being disclosed as a separate item, then there is little to do but go along with that decision. The problem which now arises is that the company must reveal, for each provision, the aggregate amount at the beginning and end of the year, any amounts which have been transferred to or from the provision during the financial year, and, more importantly, the source and application of those transfers.

On the surface this might appear to blow any chance of a company keeping secret the purposes of and movements on a specific provision. However, there is an escape route from this baring-all scenario. It comes in the shape of that dreadful five lettered word — 'other'. No doubt when the word was first invented, perhaps in some Stone Age Scrabble game, its creator did not realise what a favour he was doing for the creative accountants who, centuries later, would be acting out their own version of rubbing two stones together, aided and abetted by that random selection of five letters which were thrown so conveniently together.

For although the Companies Act says that an analysis must be provided for each provision, it has no objection, it seems, to a collective category of 'other provisions'. It is within this category that a company will be able to hide its more sensitive provisions, although it will then become more difficult to disguise the ways in which it has used these as a profits smoothing mechanism. The best way around this problem is for the company to hide any write-backs to the profit and loss account amongst the amount disclosed, in the analysis in the notes to the accounts, as being utilised in the year. This is probably more effective than netting the write backs against any charges to the profit and loss account. It should be pointed out, though, that while the 'other provisions' escape route should be available to cope with most situations, the law insists that any individual provision contained therein which is itself material, should be disclosed separately. The decision on whether or not an item is material is, of course, arbitrary, and therefore a company will usually be able to retain anonymity.

So although the overall disclosure requirements make the creative accountant's job that little bit harder, there is still sufficient flexibility within the rules on both creditors and debtors to allow some gentle massaging of the figures. It has to be remembered that the disclosure rules apply only to the company's published accounts, which appear some weeks after the preliminary announcement of profits for the year. Given that it is this announcement which is going to affect the share price and be examined by City analysts, then the manipulation should still achieve the desired effect, even though it might be later uncovered by a closer review of the annual accounts.

This says more about the workings of the City than it does about the relevance of company accounts, but it emphasises the importance for shareholders and potential investors to scrutinise the published financial statements when they finally appear. A careful examination of the detailed notes on both debtors and creditors should give at least a broad indication of how the company has used these areas to play around with its reported profit. The accounts have to provide a better basis for taking a considered view of the company's prospects than an often sparse preliminary announcement.

11

HOW to SMARTEN STOCK

Stock is the only item which appears both in a company's balance-sheet and its profit and loss account. This privileged position makes it potentially the most important aspect of a company's business and this is reflected in the sleepless nights and sweaty palms which bedevil auditors whenever they have to deal with it. The audit of stock is undertaken with the same fear, care and apprehension which is normally found amongst bomb disposal experts. There is always this worry that the value attributed to the stock will blow up in the auditor's face, taking him and the company with it.

That concern is not without justification. The margin for error is vast. And the errors can be caused for innumerable reasons. It may be straightforward creative accounting, it may be simply unintentional or it may even be the function of total malice aforethought. The problem is compounded by the fact that the nature of stock and hence its valuation varies widely from company to company and from industry to industry. It is hard to imagine a farm's stock sharing much in common with that of an advertising agency. Yet both types of business will have an item in their accounts relating to stock and work in progress. It is little wonder that when the ASC launched its standard on how to deal with the subject in 1975 it was moved to say: 'No area of accounting has produced wider differences in practice than the computation of the amount at which stock and work in progress are stated in financial accounts.' More than a decade later nothing has happened to change that position.

It follows then that the scope for creative accounting is extensive. However, it will vary depending on the nature of the company's operations. This chapter, therefore, deals with the underlying principles involved rather than the specific practices which will be appropriate in one industry but perhaps not in another. For the same reason no analysis is provided of the special circumstances which relate to long term contract work in progress found mainly in the construction industry. Still, the basic themes which underpin creative accounting in the area of stock and work in progress are common to all industries, and should provide a sufficient overview for preparers and users of accounts alike to establish the key areas to which attention should be paid.

At this stage it is useful to examine just what the accounting and legal requirements relating to stock are. The basic rule set out in Statement of Standard Accounting Practice 9 is that stock should be valued at the lower of cost or net realisable value. Company law dictates that a business may use a variety of methods in arriving at the purchase price or production cost of stocks. However, if this value is materially different from the replacement cost of those stocks, then this and the amount should be disclosed. Cost, according to the accounting rules, is: 'The expenditure which has been incurred in the normal course of business in bringing the product or service to its present location and condition. This expenditure should include, in addition to cost of purchase such costs of conversion as are appropriate to that location and condition.' It is this last part of the definition which presents the real creative accounting opportunities.

Those three little words 'costs of conversion' mean so much. It is they which allow a company to include, as part of its stock valuation, an element of production overheads. This of course requires an arbitrary system of allocation which effectively permits the company to charge, within reason, whatever it likes to its stock account. This is particularly important at the year end. The effect is not just to boost the value of the asset recorded in the profit and loss account but also to increase profits for the year. This is illustrated by a simple example. Two companies, A and B, in the same business, both have annual sales of £100 million. Both have the same opening stock and purchases of material in the year but put different values on the closing stock. The cost of those sales is thus opening stock of £10 million plus the purchases during the year of £50 million less the closing stock which Company A values at £20 million and Company B values at £15 million. The effect of the different value attributed to the year end stock is as follows.

	Company A		Company B	
	£m	£m	£m	£m
Sales		100		100
Less: cost of sales Opening Stock	10		10	
Purchases	50		50	
Closing Stock	(20)		(15)	
		40		45
Gross Profit		60		55

Company A turns in a profit £5 million better than that achieved by Company B simply by inflating the value of the year end stock. It will also have the benefit of an additional £5 million of assets in its balance-sheet, because the attributable cost of the stock will still be less than the net realisable value when it is sold off as a finished product. Yet this anomaly is fairly typical of the kind of problem which is difficult to avoid when arbitrary assessments and judgements are applied in order to arrive at some kind of valuation.

You need only look at the International Accounting Standard which deals with the valuation of stock. It cites the following stock valuation methods as being some — the word *some* should be stressed — of the approaches currently used in practice: first in first out, weighted average cost, last in first out, basic stock, specific indexation, next in first out and latest purchase price. In out, in out, shake it all about, you do the year end stock-take and you change the sums, that's what it's all about. With such a wide variety of choices available it is hardly surprising that stock valuations sometimes seem to be carried out with the same sense of order as a rather drunken version of the Hokey Cokey.

As long as a company can demonstrate that a particular method is the most appropriate for its operations and activities, then there is little to prevent its use. In practice, the accountancy profession prefers to limit companies to a choice between the first in first out method of stock valuation, and the weighted average price method. Even this limited choice still throws up a wide variation in the resulting valuations.

Companies A and B again have the same opening stocks with the same value, make identical purchases in the year and have the same number of units in stock at the year end. Company A uses the weighted average method of calculating its year end stock value while Company B adopts the first in first out approach. The details of the stock transactions are as follows:

		units	value £
Opening Stock		200	1,000
Purchases	January	100	600
	March	50	400
	June	200	2,000
	August	100	1,300
	December	150	1,700
Year End Stock		350	?

Company A, using the weighted average method, would value year end stock by pricing each unit held at that time at the average cost of units purchased in the year and held at the start. That average price was £8.75 (800 units costing £7,000), which gives a total valuation for year end stock of £3,062.50 (350 units at £8.75). Company B, using the first in first out method, values its year end stock on the basis that it is the latest purchases which remain in stock at the year end. The value attributed is therefore that relating to the cost of all the August and December purchases plus half that of the June consignment. This gives a stock valuation of £4,000 (£1,700 + £1,300 + £1,000).

Even from this simple example it is immediately apparent that the two methods bring widely differing stock valuations. Company B's stock is valued at nearly one third higher than that of Company A's, yet both businesses have had exactly the same transactions in the year at the same prices and have ended up with exactly the same stock levels. This discrepancy is caused by the fact that the example assumes that the cost of the purchases has been rising in the year. If prices had remained constant throughout the year then there would have been no difference in the stock valuations irrespective of the measurement method adopted. It follows that if a company wants to carry forward a higher year end stock value, then the first in first out method should be used in times of rising prices, and the weighted average method in times of falling prices.

The onus is on the management to adopt a method of stock valuation which is a realistic approximation to the actual stock incurred. The company auditor would expect the method to be regularly reviewed and, although eyebrows might be raised if changes to the policy used were instituted on a fairly regular basis simply to take advantage of price fluctuations, there is still a substantial element of flexibility. It is only when a company tries to take more than its fair share of unrealised profit, by valuing stocks at replacement cost in times of rising prices, that the auditors start to get a little worried. Ironically, the requirement of the Companies Act, that material differences between the stated stock valuation and its replacement cost be disclosed, is almost an incentive for a company to use the higher valuation; although stocks might then be reported at a higher amount than their actual cost.

However, these methods only relate to the value which is attributable to the cost of the purchases the company makes. The accounting rules, you will recall, also insist that costs of conversion be included as part of the year end stock. It is the allocation of these overheads and other production costs which gives rise to considerable scope for manipulation of the reported stock. There are two main problems. The first relates to the identification of those overheads, which are genuinely part of the cost of conversion of the stock. The second is concerned with the suitability of the costing systems which a company uses in order to arrive at a realistic apportionment of the overheads.

Some costs and overheads are immediately identifiable as being directly related to the process of converting bought-in stocks into a state where they are suitable for onward sale or processing. Direct labour costs, direct production expenses and the fixed production overheads are clearly all part of the conversion process. Similarly, costs relating to the supervision and management of production, quality control expenses, and items such as insurance, rates and depreciation can be justifiably treated as part of the costs of conversion. The problems arise with the allocation of central costs and overheads which are not obviously linked to production. It could be argued, for instance, that the company's general management team, particularly in smaller organisations, is actively involved in supervising the production process, and therefore an element of the related costs should be attributed to year end stock as part of the costs of conversion. The same problem will arise with central service departments such as the accounts or personnel sections.

The basic rule is that overheads should be classified according to their distinguishing characteristics. The salary of the production manager is therefore a cost of production, while that of the marketing manager is not. However, it is obvious that there are many overheads where that distinction is far from clear, and it is in these grey areas that some subtle manipulation of the stock figure can be carried out. It is only at the year end that the problem arises, since this is when the stock is being carried forward, taking an element of effectively deferred expenditure with it. The cost is not avoided altogether since the closing stocks in one year are, of course, the opening stocks of the next, and will therefore be included as part of that year's cost of sales.

There is another identification problem relating to overheads. This centres on the distinction between what are normal and what are abnormal costs. The accounting rules on stock conversion and valuation are designed to recognise only the usual recurring costs of production. Any costs which are incurred as a result of one-off incidents or events should not strictly be accounted for as part of the conversion process, but charged separately to reflect their exceptional nature. So if a batch of stock is accidently spoiled because of a mishap in the workshop, that cost should be strictly written off straight to the profit and loss account, rather than included in the stock valuation. Again, though, the decision on whether something is a normal part of the production process or a one-off event is arbitrary in nature. The lack of any hard and fast rules therefore makes it quite easy for a rather liberal overhead allocation policy to be adopted.

The effect of different approaches to the apportionment of overheads on reported profits can be large. Take the identical companies A and B with financial years ending on 31st December. Both have annual sales of £100 million, opening stocks of £30 million and a cost of sales before allowing for year end stocks of £50 million. The closing stocks are valued at £20 million before the allocation of certain central overheads and the cost of an accidental batch spoilage shortly before the year end. The central overheads amount to £24 million in the year. Company A allocates a part of these to the production process and estimates that the December costs of £2 million should be attributed to closing stock. Company B charges the central overheads to the profit and loss account as they are incurred. Similarly Company A includes the batch spoilage, which cost £5 million, as a cost of conversion and thus in its year end stock. Company B writes the spoilage off straight to the profit and loss account. The trading statements of the two companies are as follows on page 127.

The effect in this particular year is quite startling. Company A comes out with net profits which are more than twice those earned by Company B. It also carries in the balance-sheet stock which is valued at £7 million more than Company B's. This discrepancy is merely a function of the different treatments of overheads. However, do not forget that this

		Company A		Company B	
		£m	£m	£m	£m
Sales			100		100
Less:	Opening stock	30		30	
	Cost of sales	50		50	
	Closing stock	(27)		(20)	
			(53)		(60)
Gross profit			47		40
Less:	Central overheads	22		24	
	Stock spoilage	—		5	(29)
			(22)		
Net Profit			25		11

stock valuation will catch up with Company A in the following year. Its profits will at the outset be £7 million behind those of Company B, and therefore Company A will have to defer even more overheads in that year if it is to make up the difference. This knock-on effect cannot be ignored. It is easy sometimes to overlook this factor, and a company must take into account the longer term considerations when assessing its overhead allocation policy. However, as a means of making up for a short term decline in trading which can be made up in the following year, a clever use of overhead allocation can be very effective.

For companies where the business does not have a production process, the scope for manipulation might be more restricted. Even so, central overheads are a common feature in all businesses, and therefore there is some room for manoeuvre when they are allocated.

It is more important that, a company, and therefore its shareholders, should be aware of the opportunities which overhead allocation offers for smoothing out those unwanted profits fluctuations. This is by far and away its best use as a creative accounting tool. Any abuse will only put undue pressure on the trading performance of future years and will ultimately aggravate the company's auditors unnecessarily.

The difficulties with the allocation of overheads is not just related to a proper identification. Confusion can also be generated by the cost and overhead absorption system which the management uses. There are countless systems which are generally categorised as aspects of management accounting. A whole range of budgetary controls and variance analysis systems might be employed; be they standard cost, marginal cost, full cost or zero based budgeting systems the purpose is essentially to allow the management some degree of control over the expenses of production. These systems are too complex and too varied in their nature to explore in any detail. However, each will be subject to the same type of uncertainty that arises when the assumptions on which the systems are based become no longer appropriate. This can lead to distortions and discrepancies which the accountancy rules are keen to avoid. These dictate that the system which is used as the basis for overhead allocation to year end stocks should be based on the company's normal level of activity. Some managers may argue that there is no such thing as a normal level of activity, but the accountancy profession does not let things like that stand in the way of a sound and solid principle.

If the company's management is not entirely sure what is meant by the normal level of activity, the ASC has some suggestions to help them out. The rules suggest that, as a starting-point, some attention might be paid to the volume of production which was intended by the designers, and indeed the management, when the facilities were first set up, given the working conditions and shift systems which prevailed during the year.

This is a fine idea in principle but the intentions when a factory was first built or a workshop set up might well have been overtaken by events outside the company's control, resulting in a reassessment of the position. To cope with this, the appendix to the accounting standard dealing with stocks suggests that attention should also be paid to the budgeted levels of activity for the year under review and ensuing years. Attention should also be paid to the levels of activity which are actually achieved in the year, and how this compares with previous years. All this attention is being paid with such studious care for one simple purpose — to make sure that any unused capacity is written off in the year in which it wasn't used.

As many companies have found to their cost, they are positioned in industries which suffer from chronic over-capacity. Clearly this has very serious long term implications for the viability of the individual companies and in some cases, the industry itself. However, it also poses some short term problems in how to account for the overheads which relate to the unused element of a company's capacity. The extent of the difficulty is easy to see if you imagine a fixed overhead of £100 which relates to a production line designed to make 100 units a year when operating at full capacity: the attributable overhead is £1 a unit. However, if the company's business suffers and the production line only operates at half capacity, the 50 units produced then attract an overhead of £2 a unit, double that under full capacity. The question arises as to whether the extra £1 should be carried forward as part of the year end stock valuation or written off as a cost for the year?

Clearly the answer will affect the stock valuation and of course reported profits for the year. On the same principle demonstrated in the overhead identification example, the more overhead which is included in stock the higher its value and the higher the profits for the year. It is always going to be difficult to form a firm conclusion on what is represented by normal activity, and therefore the best that the company's auditors can hope for is that they will be able to form a view on the chosen system's reasonableness. That reasonableness offers enormous potential for manipulation.

There are two main thrusts to the creative accounting which can be carried out in this area. The first, which is perhaps more limited, is to toy around with the company's normal operating capacity. By assuming a lower level of activity than is anticipated, a company will be able to attribute a higher level of overheads to each item of stock which could assist in boosting the year end stock valuation, although there is a danger of over absorption. The drawback with this is that the company's auditors are likely to insist on some element of consistency in the view which is taken on what constitutes normal activity. The accounting standard quite graciously acknowledges that there are such things as variances and short term fluctuations, but it does not tolerate habitual offenders. The standard states: 'Although temporary changes in the load of activity may be ignored, persistent variations should lead to a revision of the previous norm.' This may give the company sufficient flexibility to overcome its own short term problems, but it does limit the opportunities to repeat the tactic at a later date.

A better method of tampering with the year end stock valuations is to manipulate the actual level of manufacturing operations. These can be speeded up or slowed down towards the year end, or the time of the annual stocktaking, if this takes place at a different time, to influence the physical levels of stôck which a compnay has at the year end. This is perhaps more an example of creative management than creative accounting, but the effect is still the same. The stock position at the end of the company's year is artificially inflated or deflated. It may be particularly appropriate for those companies which, because of tight year end reporting deadlines imposes by an overseas parent, have to carry out a physical stock check before the end of the year and then adjust forward for the outstanding months.

Again, it must be remembered that excessive abuse of the overhead allocation system can eventually catch up with a company. However, some judicious management and careful allocation of the relevant costs can help enormously in the profits smoothing process. The same is true of the attitude which is taken to any inefficiencies in the production process. The position here is similar to that of the one-off incidents, such as the stock spoilages mentioned in the example on overhead identification. Once again there is an incentive for a company to include the cost of any production inefficiencies in the year end stock valuation rather than to write them off in the year in which they occurred. The implications of carrying forward the cost of these shortfalls as part of stock are exactly the same as for any other type of overhead.

So far the discussion of stock has centred on the cost which should be attributed to it for year end valuation purposes. However, you will remember that the basic accounting rule is that stock should be reported in the accounts at the lower of cost or net realisable value. The implication of this is that where the stock is worth less than what it cost to buy or produce, it should be valued at what it could be sold off for, if anything. This basis will be appropriate for those items which have been damaged, have become obsolete, or, because of their slow moving nature, might have to be sold at a knock down price.

Once again the decision on whether an item's value has fallen below its cost is arbitrary in nature, and therefore requires the subjectivity which is the lifeblood of the creative accountant. It has to be pointed out that in some situations the write-down of an item of stock to below its cost cannot be avoided, particularly when it is a question of physical deterioration or damage. In these cases it would not only be breaking the accounting rules to avoid the write-off, but it also constitutes imprudent management.

However, when the decision has to be taken on the grounds of obsolescence, or because items are slow-moving, there is much more flexibility. Again though, failure to recognise that some parts of the inventory have fallen in value below their original cost may result in longer term difficulties. Where this has happened the fact must be accounted for at some stage, and perhaps the best that can be done is for the provision to be deferred to a later period.

One way round the problem of ugly blemishes in the shape of large write-downs is to make a regular provision for obsolete, damaged and slow-moving stocks. The disadvantage of this is that it represents an annual charge to profits. However, it does have the distinct plus point of bringing an element of consistency to the proceedings. The level of the annual provision can be established by reference to a particular formula. It may be simply a percentage of the total year end value of the stock, or it could be calculated on some other appropriate basis.

The provision can also be used as a very effective smoothing tool. By making overly prudent provisions in years of plenty, a company then has the flexibility either to do away with the write-down provision in the years of famine or, in the very lean years, actually to write some of the provision back to help boost year end stock. However, using an annual provision method of accounting for stock obsolescence does not excuse a company from maintaining a close watch over the actual state of the inventory. If a regular and realistic assessment of the stock is not made, it can lead to the provision getting totally out of line. This is contrary to the general objective of avoiding fluctuations. The company will want to avoid making any unusual write-downs or write-backs which will only serve to attract the stock market's attention and won't go down too well with the auditors either, since they will have been happily approving the level of provisions which had been made in previous years. Consistency is fine and commendable until a company realises that it has been consistently wrong, and that embarrassing adjustments are called for.

Any business which is involved in large purchases of raw materials, which are dependent on the commodity or other independently fluctuating markets for their price, will have to pay particular attention to the net realisable value question. Some inopportune purchasing policies or a sudden decline in the open market price of a particular commodity can cause problems. Generally it should be possible to avoid having to make significant provisions to reflect the vagaries of the market place, but a permanent decline in prices or plain old inefficient purchasing may require write-downs, and it is important for the company, therefore, to be well aware of the movements in commodity prices, so that the year end approach to the stock valuation can be tailored to mask these unfortunate and perhaps unusual circumstances.

For companies where the levels of the stocks do not perhaps justify an annual provision, the approach to write-offs will be tempered by the stock position in a particular year. Once again the objective must be to maintain a realistic value for stock, but to do so in a way which does not result in wild fluctuations. This means that a careful balancing exercise might have to be carried out, which is designed on the one hand to boost the stock valuation in preparation for reducing it again, and on the other in the shape of a write-down. There may well be a case for deferring some provisions until the next accounting period if to take all the appropriate write-offs in the same year would bring a sharp reduction in the stock valuation. All the time the creative accountant will be fully aware of the importance of maintaining a steady progression in the company's stock profile.

However, all the work of the creative accountant is rendered useless if the company does not have an effective and efficient control over its stock and its stock taking procedures. If the physical stock is already being tampered with lower down in the organisation, then the chances of senior management retaining a firm grip on its own manipulation measures are much reduced. It has to be remembered that for many businesses, its stock is in a readily realisable condition, and is therefore something of a target for light-fingered employees. There are many examples of fraud, in varying degrees of size and complexity, which have been linked directly with the company's stock, and the management's failure to maintain adequate control over it.

One example of a highly effective fraud involving the theft of stock came from a building supplies company, which had a number of branches spread around the country, each controlled by a manager who had responsibility for stock taking procedures at his branch. At one of the biggest branches a junior manager, who had a taste for fast women and slow horses, decided that the only way to keep himself in the style to which his girlfriends and bookmaker had become accustomed, was to indulge in a little private enterprise. In effect, he set up his own small business which unfortunately relied entirely on his employer's stock for its existence. Without wishing to cast a slur on the building industry in general, there are some elements of it which would look more at home firing six shooters in the air, sporting ten-gallon hats and chasing after a posse of Sioux indians.

These cowboys who deal only in discounts for cash and who think VAT is an abbreviation for Vodka and Tonic, provided the customer base for the enterprising junior manager. Nods and winks were exchanged for fistfuls of used fivers, and the company's stock quietly found its way out of the warehouse and into the back of Ford Transit vans of dubious road worthiness and even more dubious ownership. However, the fraudster was well aware of the implications of his dirty deeds. It was he who effectively ran the branch accounts since the senior manager had little interest in this rather mundane and boring task. He was also largely responsible for overseeing the annual stocktake, and realised that the missing stock would be detected when the branch's gross profit margin was analysed. He therefore maintained very careful records of the stock which left by the back door under the cover of darkness.

To compensate for the stolen stock he then placed empty boxes, which would previously have contained high value items, around the warehouse in the most awkward of places. Had the boxes been full then their value would have equated roughly to that of the absentee items. At the time of the annual stock take, which always took place on New Year's Eve with opening time beckoning, the junior manager made sure that nobody got too close to the empty boxes and they were duly counted on the assumption that they were full. The fraud worked perfectly year in year out. The gross margins were maintained and everybody was happy. However, the branch's business eventually outgrew the size of the warehouse and a bigger and better home was found for it.

It was at this stage that the junior manager came well and truly unstuck. The move into the new home was planned for New Year's Eve so that it would coincide with the stock take, thus allowing two birds, and as it transpired a thief, to be killed with one stone. The size of the move, and the company's pride in its new bigger branch, resulted in a swarm of head-office staff coming down to help out with the task. The poor junior manager looked on aghast as eager pasty-faced clerks from the accounts department gleefully and innocently crumpled up the occasional empty box with the enthusiasm often found in those who only have to undertake manual work for the one day. As the day wore on the mound of flattened cardboard boxes grew higher, still without attracting too much attention. It was only when the stock taking was completed and the valuation carried out that the full significance of the empty boxes and the enormity of the crime became apparent. A gross margin which had been steadily maintained at around 20 per cent crumbled to a little over 6 per cent, when an accurate closing stock figure was used in the calculation for the first time in some years.

The junior manager had no choice but to come clean. He did not quite break down in tears wailing: 'It's a fair cop but society is to blame', but he was sufficiently penitent and the company's embarrassment was sufficiently great for him to get away with little more than instant dismissal. It is a cautionary tale for all companies. They should always be aware that their innocent manipulation of stock at head-office might be being imitated and undermined by some altogether more sinister manipulation elsewhere in the organisation.

It is not just fraudsters who threaten to destroy the company's carefully planned pattern of smooth growth. In-effecient managers who are conscious that they are not meeting performance targets might also be tempted to indulge in a little creative accounting of their own. The sensitive nature of stock and the ease with which it can be manipulated makes it an obvious target for artificial adjustment which will make a poor financial performance, well below budget, become much more palatable. The difficulty is that, while all appears to be going well and targets seem to be being met quite comfortably, there is a danger that the senior management will leave the individual branch or subsidiary to its own devices with only minimum supervision. However, the number of provisions which appear in company accounts relating to 'stock write-downs at a subsidiary' suggests that the hands-off approach to management is not always appropriate. The senior management must, therefore, be prepared to relinquish their role as creative accounting poachers and occasionally take on the unfamiliar mantle of gamekeeper.

If effective control over the individual company and branch assets is maintained, then the task of implementing smoothing measures at the group level is made that much easier. The opportunities for creativity in the area of stock and work in progress is just too good to be ruined by slip-ups elsewhere. It is another variation on the theme of looking after the pennies and letting the pounds look after themselves. But stock is not only an area of great scope for manipulation, it is also an area where the chances of the outside world finding out exactly what you have been up to are remote to say the least.

This becomes apparent from a cursory glance at the ways in which companies disclose their accounting policy on stocks and work in progress. The accounts of Blue Circle Industries, the cement group, for the year ended 31st December 1984, state quite simply that: 'The basis of valuation is the lower of cost and net realisable value. Cost includes direct costs and appropriate overheads.' This policy is mirrored almost exactly by that of the Hawley Group, the cleaning to security services company. Its accounts for the same year reveal that: 'Stocks are valued at the lower of cost and net realisable value. Cost includes an addition for overheads where appropriate.'

Neither policy goes out of its way to inform shareholders of the specific bases and assumptions which have been applied in establishing the stock valuation. However, Blue Circle and Hawley are not alone in their reluctance to go into too much detail. The 1984–85 Survey of UK Published Accounts, published by the Institute of Chartered Accountants in England and Wales, revealed that the level of disclosure of the methods of costing stocks was very low. Of the companies whose accounts were analysed in the survey, some 73 per cent gave no indication of the method which had been employed in arriving at the cost of stock. There was a better showing on the disclosure of whether or not overheads had been included as part of the stock valuation. Even so, 30 per cent of the companies in the survey failed to make any statement on the treatment of overheads. The lack of detailed disclosure makes it very difficult for shareholders, and other users of accounts, to establish with any certainty how the company has gone about its stock valuation.

The absence of information may not be intentional, but there is no doubt that it does no harm to a company if it gives away as little as possible on its stock valuation policy, and retains a shroud of uncertainty behind which it can make the necessary refinements to the approach adopted as and when required. There is no overt pressure on companies to improve this aspect of their financial accounts, and in its absence few companies will go out of their way to make improvements voluntarily.

It is a sad fact that few shareholders pay too much attention anyway to a company's accounting policies. This is regrettable, since this is the closest that the company ever comes to revealing how it has arrived at the figures which are contained in the accounts. Perhaps a greater interest from shareholders might provoke an improvement in the standard of accounting policy disclosure from the companies they own. Many accounting policies are couched in such vague and often garbled terms that they probably restrict rather than improve any understanding of the business. However, while the companies and their shareholders happily co-habit in a world of mutual disinterest in accounting policies, there is little prospect of an improvement.

Perhaps if shareholders were aware of the kind of accounting tricks which are carried out in arriving at the stock valuation, then they might be encouraged to take more than their current passing interest in the underlying policies.

12

HOW to BRUSH UP BORROWINGS and CASH

Cash is king. Ever since the barter economy gave way to one based on an exchangeable currency, money has made the world go around. It has become the life-blood of every company. A surfeit of liquid funds is an indication of success, a surfeit of debt is an indication of failure. A business can play around as much as it likes with the value of its other assets and liabilities but when the money runs out then its days are numbered. Redundancy provisions can be charged above the line or below the line, they can be deferred or brought forward, but if the cash isn't there to pay the sacked workers their entitlement when they leave, the other issues become completely irrelevant. Income can be recognised at whatever time the company chooses, but if it never actually receives the cash, it can start counting the days it has left for this world.

It is because of this importance that a company's cash and or borrowings presents only the most limited scope for creative accounting. Other areas of the balance-sheet and profit and loss account are granted their opportunities for creativity because of the absence of a firm relationship between them and actual cash payments. Further, these areas are open to large amounts of subjective assessment and assumption which is clearly not available when dealing with cash. A bank will not take very kindly to a company deciding that the £1 million it owes will be written down to a mere £100,000. The only way that the £1 million can be reduced is for the company to repay its debt.

Given this constraint and the clear importance of a company's liquidity, it is not surprising that the scope for creative accounting is here quite rightly restricted.

Ironically, the closest a set of accounts comes to producing a crucial analysis of cash flow is the statement of sources and applications of funds, yet it is given only minimal attention by most companies, the accountancy profession and indeed shareholders and other users. This statement aside, there is little in the financial statements to indicate the company's cash position apart from a year end on year end comparison of the cash and borrowings position. This of course has its limitations as an indicator of cash flow, since the balance-sheet is no more than a photograph of the company's state of affairs at a given point in time. A better indication comes from the amount of interest which has been paid or received in the year, although this of course is influenced by the rates which have applied during the period.

It is this limitation on the outsiders' ability to assess the real cash flow of the business which offers the best opportunity for any creativity. By and large that opportunity is restricted to a subtle use of disclosure, and, to a lesser extent, the control of cash flows which is more akin to the largely discredited window-dressing. There are of course innumerable off balance-sheet financing schemes now available, and these are discussed in greater detail in a separate chapter.

At a first glance the rules on disclosure do not offer a tremendous amount of room for manouevre. The basic principle laid down in the Companies Acts is that no set-off between assets and liabilities is permitted. The implication is that cash balances cannot be offset against borrowings to reduce the overall group position.

However, a closer analysis of the law's wording suggest that there are certain situations where some element of netting off will be allowed. This is because the law does not actually define what it means by liability, and it can be argued that a suitable definition would be one based on the amount which a company would have to pay if legal proceedings were taken against it to recover monies owing. Under that definition there will be several situations where netting off could be allowed. These situations all assume that cash deposits and borrowings are arranged with the same bank and by the same company. Thus, cash deposited by one subsidiary could not be offset against borrowings by another, unless specific criteria are met.

Netting off will, therefore, be allowed in situations where cash deposited and cash borrowed are done so under similar conditions, such as where the relevant sums are due for payment on demand or on the same date. Group balances could be offset on consolidation in situations where all the subsidiaries agreed that they were jointly or severally liable to the bank for the amounts owing, and similarly the bank accepted that it had a joint and several liability to repay deposits.

The benefits of netting off for a company is that the total level of debt which the group has is masked by the inclusion of cash balances. So a company which has not used netting off before might be able to do so on a selective basis in a particular year, in order to give the impression that it has not been borrowing as much money as would otherwise be indicated in its financial statements.

However, netting off has its limitations. When the City is assessing a group's level of gearing, it bases its calculations on the company's net borrowings position. There is no immediate benefit, in terms of influencing this all-important ratio, which is regarded very much as an indication of financial stability. The company must therefore rely on the timing of its cash payments and receipts if it is to succeed in manipulating its cash and borrowings position.

For companies which are highly geared, that is to say, with large net borrowings positions, the aim will be to defer cash payments at the year end until the next accounting period. The company will defer making payments to creditors in an effort to inflate artificially the cash position. One of the favourite methods of window-dressing is to write out cheques for creditor payments but not to send the cheques out. All over the country around the time of the year end there are large bundles of cheques sitting in finance directors' drawers waiting to be sent out. This rather unsubtle method of reducing the level of creditors, while keeping bank balances in a better light, very rarely works these days. Even the most unsophisticated of auditing firms is well aware of the trick. However, variations on that scheme can still work. Providing the cheques are not actually written out then certain liabilities can be disclosed as part of creditors rather than as a bank overdraft, which will clearly help the year end cash position. Any payment over which the company has an element of control is a reasonable target for deferral. Things like staff bonuses or redundancy payments should, if possible, be delayed until the next accounting period.

The counter to this is to bring forward cash receipts into the current accounting period. This is obviously more difficult. Since many companies share common year ends, it follows that, if everybody is trying to delay making payments, collecting cash early is easier said than done. However, a closer than usual attention to debt collection will reap its benefits, particularly if the process is stepped up two or three months rather than two or three days before the year end.

The year end cash position can also be improved by a much more ruthless approach to stock control as the accounting period draws to its inevitable conclusion. It is easy to overlook how much cash can be tied up in excessively, and unnecessarily, high levels of stock. A gradual run down of stocks will inevitably free up cash, athough care must be taken that this does not result in damaging shortages. However, such methods of improving the cash position owe more to careful and prudent management than to creative accounting.

But not all businesses have the problem of excessive gearing to cope with. Remember, a prudent level of borrowing is often looked upon as being a sign of good management. High cash balances can be regarded as a waste of a company's resources. When similar companies are earning a return of 20 per cent on their assets and another company has large amounts of cash stashed away in the building society, then City analysts and company shareholders alike begin to wonder why. Thus there can be an incentive for a company to give the impression that its year end cash position is not as healthy as it really is.

The methods employed in such a situation are the exact opposite of those used when a company is trying to inflate its year end cash position. Payments are accelerated and, if possible, debtors are invited to delay their payments which they will normally be happy to do. The motive does not have to derive from the wish to reduce the level of net cash disclosed in the balance sheet; it may own more to the need to smoothe out cash flows. If a company has had a year of unusually positive cash flow, perhaps because of an unavoidable delay in a particular capital investment which will not take place until the next accounting period, it may not necessarily want this distortion to be reflected in the accounts. Once again the company's objective will be to remove unusual fluctuations, and demonstrate that it has a steadily improving cash flow profile. It will not want to have a one-off benefit to its net cash position in one year, which will be immediately removed in the next simply as a function of the timing of a particular capital investment.

However, the year end position is not the only indicator of the company's cash flow. The interest paid or received in the year will give a further indication of the level of average borrowings. Here again there is not a tremendous amount of scope for creative accounting, and the emphasis is much more on good treasury management. There are tremendous savings which can be made by a company if it keeps a close eye on the money markets, and, if it has overseas transactions to deal with, then an eye on the foreign exchange markets as well. Apart from the various money market instruments which can be used, a company must also pay close attention to the way in which its borrowings are structured.

There are several ways in which the portfolio of debt can be constructed in order to reduce the level of interest payable. By combining short term borrowings with long term debt a company can secure both flexibility and competitive interest rates. It should also consider its capital structure. If long term debt is threatening to get out of hand, a company could reduce it by launching a rights issue. Such a move is not always welcomed by the stock market, particularly if the reason for it is cited just as debt reduction, and is not linked to any other long term strategic plan. Again, this is more in the domain of the corporate treasurer than the creative accountant.

The same is true of money market instruments, such as futures and swaps, which can be used either as means of speculation or hedging. However, the money markets are highly competitive places and are no place for the casual player or inexperienced trader. Unless the company's treasury needs are big enough to justify a separate department these matters might be better left to the experts, although this does not preclude simple measures such as placing large cash sums on overnight deposit. The benefits from internal treasury management can be substantial as BP discovered when it set up its own bank to handle the company's finances. In a short space of time it was earning millions of pounds of additional profit for the organisation, simply by devoting specific resources to the task. True, not every company has the same size of business as BP, nor such a wide variety of transactions, but even on a more reduced scale the benefits which accrue through good treasury management will not be insignificant.

More companies are beginning to take advantage of the corporate bond market which can allow a business in effect to take an interest rate holiday. By using stepped interest bonds, which are loans with escalating rates of interest, over a period of time, a company can reduce its interest burden in earlier years, which is normally when such relief is most needed.

Safeway UK, the British arm of the supermarket division, showed considerable imagination when it combined a deep discount with stepped interest rates to raise a £100 million in 1985. The deep discount made it attractive to investors who would only receive 3 per cent interest at the outset, rising in stages every five years to 8.25 per cent by the year 2011. The equivalent yield for investors was, therefore, quite competitive, and also tax efficient. For Safeway the benefits accrue from the interest holiday it has earned for itself.

There are other ways which a company can set about improving its cash position without resorting to the sophistication of the money markets and without devoting huge amounts of time and resources to the subject. One of the most effective methods is to make greater use of leased assets. This does not involve a high capital outlay which would have to be financed out of the company's internal resources. It has become less attractive as a means of off balance-sheet financing since the introduction of an accounting standard which insists on the disclosure of the leased asset and the related liability. However, it still has some attractions, in that the stream of lease payments can be established with some certainty, and will not be subject to the kind of fluctuations that would arise if the asset had been financed out of borrowings, which have varying interest rates.

A variation on this theme is the use of sale and leaseback arrangements, which are much more appropriate for the creative accountant to consider. Normally such schemes will be linked to a company's freehold property. That building is likely to be quite a valuable asset, and its worth will have increased substantially. In order to realise that capital gain, and, at the same time, free up liquid funds for use elsewhere in the business, the company agrees to sell the building company either to a property company or some institutional investor. The purchaser hands over a lump sum and also agrees to lease the property straight back to its former owner. The advantage for the purchaser is that it has an immediate and guaranteed rental stream while the company keeps its home, gets a large chunk of cash and reclassifies the asset from freehold to leasehold.

Certainly the value of that asset as disclosed in the balance-sheet will be much reduced — to zero if it is an operating leaseback — but the company's borrowings will also be reduced bringing down gearing and reducing the interest bill. The rental payments which will now be incurred are hidden away amongst the company's other operating costs, and removed from the separately disclosed and closely scrutinised interest charge.

However, sale and leaseback arrangements are not always the most popular means of reducing borrowings and interest. There is something of an air of an action of last resort about them. Again though, any adverse reaction against such a move within the City is likely to be short term in nature and might even be regarded quite positively, if the leaseback means that the likelihood of the company launching a rights issue is reduced.

There is a more subtle way of reducing interest and this also involves the largest element of creative accounting. It goes under the name of capitalisation of interest, and is a fairly recent arrival on the scene. However, it is a tactic which is likely to spread in terms of popularity. Quite simply, a company treats the interest on that element of borrowings which are employed to finance the construction of fixed assets as part of the cost of those assets. One of the pioneers of interest capitalisation was BOC. In its accounting policies it declares that: 'Interest costs incurred during the construction period on major fixed asset additions are capitalised and form part of the total asset cost. Depreciation is charged on total cost, including such interest on the bases set out above.'

The note to the accounts which deals with fixed assets reveals that in the year ended 30th September 1984, the capital expenditure of the BOC Group included interest capitalised of £5 million. In the previous year that amount had been £16.1 million. The depreciation charge for the year included amortisation of previously capitalised interest of just £2.4 million, and in the year to 30th September 1983 that amortisation had been only £1 million. The net impact is quite substantial. In effect BOC boosted its reported profits in 1984 by £2.6 million (£5 million capitalised less the £2.4 million amortisation costs), and in the previous years its profits benefited to the tune of £15.1 million. At 30th September the net book value of BOC's fixed assets included £39.7 million of interest capitalised. This was just over 2 per cent of the total net book value, but is clearly a significant amount.

The pioneering work carried out by BOC has been picked up by other companies. It is becoming increasingly popular among the big supermarket chains who are committed to very costly store development programmes. The nature of the competition amongst the big food retailers dictates that the way forward is through bigger and more expensive stores.

These have gone from being supermarkets, to being hyper-markets, to being superstores, to being megastores: no one is quite sure where it will all end. The only thing that is certain is that the number of available sites is falling, while the competition to secure those sites is increasing. This pushes up the asking prices and increases the development costs which the big chains must incur. This in turn pushes up the financing requirements and the interest burden.

J Sainsbury, which has a reputation for being the country's leading retailer, led the way again, as it became the first company to start capitalising its interest costs on its store development programme. That lead was taken up by Tesco, which, despite a recent heavy rights issue to finance the stores programme, also took the interest capitalisation route. The benefits of this approach are considerable. First, both companies automatically increase their reported pre-tax profits. Second, some element of the interest escapes permanently a charge to the profit and loss account. This is because freehold land is not the subject of depreciation. So, while the interest relating to the building will ultimately be charged against profits, albeit by a much delayed amortisation cost, the interest which is allocated to the land will never actually be charged to the revenue account. Finally, by using an accounting policy which is not used by other food retailers, the likes of Sainsbury and Tesco get an unfair stock market advantage. If anything, those companies which do not capitalise interest, and actually finance store development out of their own internally generated resources, are penalised.

There is a danger that this interest capitalisation will get out of hand as the store expansion plans become more ambitious. The food retailers are effectively deferring and sometimes avoiding interest charges, even though these will have to be physically paid over to the banks which lend the money. This could lead to a misleading impression being given by them about the financial viability of the store development.

This is something about which investors must come to their own conclusions. They must decide whether the interest capitalisation is a genuine attempt to reflect the nature of the costs incurred more fairly, or whether it is merely an effort to delay bad financial news until it can be compensated for by some better news.

Just like sin, cash flow will eventually find a company out. All that interest capitalisation does is put off the day of judgement. Cash can sometimes be a very cruel king and has little mercy on those who try to abuse its power by excessive creative accounting. If ever there was a case for moderation, then it is over the way that a company accounts for and discloses its cash and borrowings position. Otherwise the cry will go up: 'Cash is dead long live the receiver.'

13

HOW to SHARPEN SHARE CAPITAL

One of the most overlooked opportunities for creative accounting lies within a company's own share capital. For many businesses the only interest in its shares stems from the price at which they are quoted on the stock exchange. They are simply instruments which can be issued to raise more money and used to finance acquisitions. The only interesting aspect of the company's shares is that their price on the stock market never reflects adequately the company's past performance and future prospects.

However, this preoccupation with the quoted price and its movements tends to prevent a company's management from picking up on the scope which now exists for taking a more active interest in its own capital. That scope is provided by the changes in company law which now make it possible for a business to buy its own shares. The opportunity to use this tactic has largely been overlooked by companies with some notable exceptions such as GEC, which has been a fairly regular buyer of its own shares.

Perhaps the problem with buying in a company's own shares is that its attractions are not immediately apparent to the company's management, or indeed to the stock market. Further, the regulations which govern how, when, and in what quantity the shares can be purchased are quite complex, and can involve the company in considerable forward planning. They also require some quite detailed explanations to be given to the shareholders, whose approval is needed before the arrangements can be put into practice.

The purchase by a company of its own shares will only be appropriate for a business which has net assets greater than the company's market capitalisation. It is traditional for shares to be quoted on the stock market at a value which is below that of the attributable value of net assets per share. There are several reasons for this. To start with, for most companies, the stock market rating is based more on the projected stream of earnings than on the assets which will create that stream. There are certain notable exceptions, such as property companies, where the value of the property portfolio has much more interest for City analysts than earnings. The general rule, though, is that the net assets of a company play second fiddle to earnings. This is understandable in the context of some of the newcomers to the Stock Exchange list. Advertising agencies, for instances, have very little to boast of in terms of tangible assets. The biggest assets are, as I have said, the people that work for the agency, and people have no tangible balance-sheet value. There will also be the case where more mature companies with a high proportion of fully depreciated assets, which are still being used to produce earnings, have a share price which is considerably higher than net assets per share.

These situations tend, however, to be the exception rather than the rule, and most companies will therefore find that their net assets are valued at more than the actual market capitalisation. It is in these situations that the purchase of own shares can be used as a means of redressing the disparity, and, at the same time, improving the share price and the earnings per share.

Take two companies of equal size and similar activity. Both have 10 million shares in issue and a share price of £5 which gives them both a market capitalisation of £50 million. The net assets of both companies are equivalent to £7 a share, which values both companies, on this basis, at £70 million. Both companies earn profits attributable to shareholders of £18 million. Company A decides that it will purchase 10 per cent of its own shares and obtains its shareholders' approval to do so. Company B refrains from taking a similar step. The effect of the different approaches is as follows.

	Company A	Company B
Shares in issue	9m	10m
Price per share	£5	£5
Market Capitalisation	£45m	£50m
Net Assets per share	£7.22	£7
Net Assets Value	£65	£70
Earnings per share	£1.94	£1.80

The illustration is based on the assumption that the purchase of Company A's own shares is made out of its own cash resources. The loss of interest on that cash is estimated to reduce attributable profits by £500,000 in the year under review.

Even after allowing for this adjustment it is clear that Company A's financial position appears to look much more attractive than that of Company B. It increases not just the value of net assets per share, but also, as part of the same transaction, increases the earnings attributable to each share.

The stock market implications of the share purchase should be to push Company A's share price higher. Its stock will now appear to be much cheaper than that of Company B. First, it has a lower price earnings ratio which implies that the shares should increase in value to reflect this. Second, Company A's shares are now at an even greater discount to net assets than they were before, which should also encourage a greater upward momentum in the price. It may also be that the very action of a big purchase of shares may prompt the market to mark the shares up simply as a reaction to the activity.

That reaction, however, will depend very much on how the market interprets the share buy-in. It may be seen as an indication that the company's management is sharp and well aware that the shares were undervalued; thus it has acted sensibly in the best interest of the shareholders by securing the stock at a substantial discount to net assets. The stock market may, in these circumstances, see the transaction as something of a bull point, and mark the shares up in recognition of this.

However, there is no guarantee that this is the reaction which will greet the buy-in. Bearing in mind that once these shares have been purchased by the company it is obliged to cancel them, the stock market may regard the action as rather futile and somewhat negative. The City might ask, with some justification, why this company is having to resort to such tactics? Could it not employ the funds used to finance the share purchase in a more constructive and perhaps more positive way?

When a company is sitting on a big pile of cash, the market is always keen to discover what plans it has for spending it. Hopes that it may be used to finance a take-over are built up, but if all the company does is buy its own shares, then these may come tumbling down. The market may begin to believe that the management is short on ideas about how to spend the cash. Might it not be better spent on developing the business? The likelihood of getting a positive reaction to the purchase of the company's own shares will be reduced if money has to be borrowed to finance the transaction. The dividend payments which are foregone will not be sufficient to offset the increased interest payments which will be incurred, and these in turn will restrict the group's cash flow. The market might also interpret the purchase as a desperate attempt to try and support a share price which has been showing signs of weakness.

However, it must be remembered that the reaction to the announcement of the share buy-in, which the company must make, will be temporary in nature. A short term fall in the price may be more than offset by the later increase which will result in the market's appreciation of the change in the fundamental factors, which affect the assessment of the share price.

It is not just share price considerations which will influence the company's decision on whether or not to go into the market to buy in its own shares. Such an action will also reflect the company's perceptions of the other commercial factors which affect its long term future and, in some cases, its long term independence.

For instance, if the management believes that there is an unwelcome predator waiting in the wings to launch a take-over bid, it may well be prudent to move in and buy up any loose shares which are floating around on the market. This reduces the opportunities for the predator to pick up those shares itself and use them as a platform to launch the bid. However, such an action may also present some longer term problems for the company to proceed with its own business development strategy, particularly if this involves an element of acquisition. Not only does the share buy-in wear down the company's liquid resources, or stretch its borrowings capabilities, but it might also suggest an element of inconsistency in the management philosophy. If the company goes into the market and buys its own shares, and then a few months later issues more shares in order to finance an acquisition, eyebrows will be raised.

However, these apparently bearish points should not deter a company from at least examining the possibility of buying its own shares. There is certainly no harm in looking, and indeed no charge for so doing. It has already been demonstrated that the company's share price can benefit considerably from such a move and this, in itself, is a sufficient incentive to review the situation. It may well be that the stock market price of the shares so undervalues the company that buying them in is simply too attractive a proposition to miss. There is certainly no harm in preparing the ground which will allow the purchase to be made, and it should be a standard policy for a company to have secured, as a matter of course, the necessary approval from shareholders to implement such a programme of action.

It is therefore essential that the company's management is well aware of the legal and other requirements which govern the purchase of its own shares. The 1985 Companies Act lays down several rules which must be adhered to. The power for a company to purchase its own shares must be embodied in its articles of association, and the incorporation of such power in those articles must be approved by the shareholders. The company must also seek approval from shareholders to proceed with a purchase of its own shares. For transactions which will be performed outside a recognised stock exchange, a special resolution must be passed; transactions which will be carried out on a recognised stock exchange need only the approval of an ordinary resolution. Such an ordinary resolution must specify the number of shares to be acquired and the maximum and minimum price which will be paid. The authority which the shareholders give to the management by way of passing this resolution lasts for a maximum of 18 months from the date of the resolution being passed. The expiry date must be specified, after which further approval from shareholders must be sought.

The accounts of GEC for the year to 31st March 1984 contained the necessary resolutions to change the articles of association and secure approval for a share buy-in. The resolution simply asked that the company be given the right to make market purchases '. . . on The Stock Exchange of up to an aggregate of 250 million ordinary shares of 5p each in its capital at not more than 300p per share and not less than 5p per share (in each case exclusive of expenses) and that the authority conferred by this resolution shall expire on 13th March 1986.'

The resolution is drafted in such a way that the company retains tremendous flexibility over the number of shares which it can purchase and at what price, but at the same time is in no way committed to make a purchase if market conditions make it an unrealistic proposition. Other companies which are considering a share buy-in would be well advised to seek a similar authority from their shareholders, even if the proposition of doing so is remote. Forward planning at an early stage relieves the company of the embarrassment of having to seek a rushed approval from share holders at a later date, which, in itself, could arouse the stock market's suspicions.

The 1985 Companies Act also specifies that only fully paid shares can be repurchased. These must then be cancelled, which in turn reduces the issued share capital. The purchase consideration for the shares bought in must be financed out of the company's profits which are available for distribution. If the shares had been issued at a premium then that premium, on a repurchase, does not, however, have to be paid for out of distributable profits, but can be offset against the appropriate element of the relevant share premium account, providing the aggregate amount of nominal capital and distributable reserves is maintained.

For shares which are repurchased entirely out of distributable profits, a transfer of an amount equal to the nominal value of those shares must be made to a capital redemption reserve. This ensures that the company's capital is maintained. Finally, the Act specifies that the purchase price must be paid on completion of the transaction.

These provisions may appear to be quite complicated but they are little more than paper adjustments, and do nothing to detract from the clear benefits which can arise through buying in the shares. However, the rules on share repurchases are not restricted to those laid down by company law. The Stock Exchange has also seen fit to weigh in with its own requirements, which, while providing additional factors to be considered by the company, are in fact less technical in nature and more related to the practical aspects of these types of transaction.

The rules only apply to listed companies and state that in any 12 month period a company can only make purchases of up to 15 per cent of its own capital. If the company wants to exceed this figure, it can only do so by way of a partial offer or tender offer. The Stock Exchange also insists that a company cannot buy its own shares in the two months which precede the announcement of its annual or half-year results. Neither of these restrictions is particularly onerous. It is unlikely that a company would want to buy in more than 15 per cent of its capital in any 12 month period. Similarly, the rule forbidding repurchases in four months of the year still allows sufficient flexibility of timing to ensure that the company can take advantage of market conditions as and when they are suited to a share buy-in.

A further consideration is the tax implications of share repurchases, which can affect their viability. Both the company's own position and that of the vendors must be examined quite closely to ensure that the transaction is carried out in the most efficient way.

Again these considerations should not act as a deterrent,

although they may be critical in determining whether the time is right to indulge in a share buy-in. Judging by the lack of activity on the share repurchasing front, perhaps it is fair to assume that companies have been put off by the various restrictions. However, by giving up so easily many businesses are missing out on a readily available creative accounting tool which, unlike many others, does not rely on a liberal interpretation of the relevant rules but is actually encouraged by them. Certainly it is not a tool which can be used too often and any abuse of it will devalue the benefits which might otherwise have been available. However, a prudent and considered use of share buy-ins can produce a considerable advantage for the company and indeed its own shareholders.

14

HOW to OPERATE OFF BALANCE-SHEET FINANCING

*T*he most effective creative accounting is that which is not detected by the independent user of company accounts. The most successful, and thereby the most sinister, methods are those which do not appear at all in the financial statements. This branch of creative accounting has become known as off balance-sheet financing. As the name suggests, this refers to the ways of raising funds for a business without reflecting those borrowings in the balance-sheet.

It is not a new phenomenon but one which is growing not just in size but also in sophistication. This off balance-sheet boom has lent an element of credibility to these methods of funding which is completely undeserved. Ironically, the initiative for the recent development of off balance-sheet finance has not come from the companies, but more from the providers of funds which have been actively marketing the schemes. This touting by the merchant banks and other financial advisers shares similarities with the peddling of artificial tax avoidance schemes in the 1970s. Again the arrangements comply with the letter of the law but are contrary to its spirit, and the justification for adopting them appears only to be that everybody else is doing the same thing.

This is no justification at all, but it has not prevented the widespread growth in off balance-sheet financing. The schemes also have some quite dangerous undertones in that they are being aggressively sold by some merchant banks in a way that suggests that they are actually an important financial service.

A merchant bank might, for instance, identify a company with high borrowings which are close to the limit imposed by its articles of association. The bank then approaches the company's management and points this out, at the same time suggesting an off balance-sheet scheme which will allow the business to increase its borrowings without breaching the articles of association. There is a strong chance that the management will be more than happy to go along with the plan, since this will relieve it of the embarrassment of having to go to the shareholders to ask for a change in the articles of association. This may be very convenient for the management, but it undermines the very reason for those articles. They would have been included to ensure that the management which runs the company on behalf of the shareholders does not overstep the mark and commit the business to unrealistic and impractical levels of debt. Thus, even this tenuous control that shareholders have over the management is eroded.

However, it is not always the limit on borrowings power which prompts a company to seek off balance-sheet finance. After all, the articles of association can, with shareholders' approval, be amended. That change will not help the management if the main problem for the business is that its borrowings are simply too high. The stock market is acutely aware of the dangers for a company which has high levels of debt that must be serviced. One of the crucial factors in assessing a company is its gearing, the proportion of net borrowings to shareholders' funds. When gearing becomes uncomfortably high, the stock market begins to get a little worried and the pressure is on the company to reduce the ratio.

When a company finds itself in the unfortunate position of having high gearing which cannot be reduced, or even held steady, out of internally generated funds, it is easy to see why the management might be lured into one of these artificial funding schemes. The off balance-sheet finance may be applied to reduce existing borrowings, thus bringing down the gearing ratio, or it may be secured in order to embark on an important project or acquisition which is needed for the company's long term future. Either way, it still represents a distortion of the company's true financial position which prevents users of the accounts obtaining a full and fair understanding of its affairs, and it may lead to an investment decision being taken on inappropriate grounds.

The position was summed up by the ASC in its foreword to Statement of Standard Accounting Practice 21, which deals with leases and hire-purchase contracts. Leasing had become a substantial source of off balance-sheet finance, and the standard was designed to recognise the substance rather than the legal form of a lease, to ensure that leased assets and the corresponding liabilities were reflected in the accounts. The ASC said: 'When a company is leasing a substantial amount of assets instead of buying them, the effect is that, unless the leased assets and obligations are capitalised, potentially large liabilities build up off balance-sheet; equally the leased assets employed are not reflected on the balance-sheet. These omissions may mislead users of a company's accounts — both external users and the company's own management.'

It was quite a bold move by the ASC. The conflict between the legal form of a transaction and its practical substance is not an easy one to resolve. However, the introduction of the leasing standard passed off without too much trouble, despite the complexity of the subject. By and large companies have been happy to capitalise the assets purchased under finance leases, and, to incorporate the corresponding liability to the lessor in the balance-sheet. There is still some uncertainty over the distinction between operating leases, which do not need to be capitalised, and the pure finance leases which must be reflected in the balance-sheet. This aside, the leasing standard must constitute something of a victory for the ASC. The question now, is whether it will be able to repeat its success in dealing with leasing on the new and more sophisticated off balance-sheet financing schemes which have sprung up more recently.

In theory, it should be possible to extend the substance

over form principle to these new schemes. However, the widespread nature of these arrangements, and the difficulty in actually identifying them, will make that task much harder. There is also a view that, if specific schemes are identified and rendered ineffective by forcing the underlying transactions back on to the balance-sheet, then all that will happen is that other more devious schemes will be developed to replace them. Perhaps the best that can be hoped for is that the general principles of off balance-sheet financing schemes can be identified, and the disclosure of their use by companies in the annual report and accounts can be improved.

Those general principles are difficult to identify. Off balance-sheet financing owes nothing to such things, and owes even less to company law. There are no rules in this particular game. Neither are there any real life examples since those indulging in off balance-sheet financing do so because they do not want anybody to know what they are really up to. It is a bit like the Russian spy who is suddenly discovered two doors down the street. He may have seemed like just another neighbour who kept himself to himself, but underneath his quiet and innocuous exterior there lurked another altogether more sinister being. It is well known, of course, that Russian spies are only ever discovered two doors down from other people; they are never discovered in your own neighbourhood. Applying the same criterion, companies in which you have an interest never indulge in off balance-sheet financing. It smacks too much of conspiracy and skullduggery, doesn't it? Or does it? The problem is that you may never know.

This is not to suggest that every company in the country is quietly involved in a series of devious schemes designed to disguise the fact that, rather than being well endowed with liquid resources, they are actually borrowed up to the hilt. The old rule that you can't fool all of the people all of the time still applies. However, there is not doubt that the flexibility of accounting rules and the rigidity of company law offers an enormous amount of scope for a business to portray its financial position in a better light. Normally this will be simply a short term measure since the providers of the off balance-sheet finance will not look kindly on their generosity being abused.

This is, in effect, a further endorsement of the underlying principle of creative accounting, which is to take evasive action in order to iron out short term fluctuations in the company's performance. It must be remembered that off balance-sheet finance, like any other kind of borrowing, has to be repaid eventually. If a business is unable to meet its commitments be they on the balance-sheet, off the balance-sheet or underneath the balance-sheet, in the long run they must be met. However, by failing to disclose the full facts about its funding methods a company which indulges in matters off balance-sheet is effectively passing the right to decide on its future prospects to the providers of the finance. Investors, creditors and others who rely on published financial data are being deprived of the full and fair information which is essential for making an informed decision.

As always, though, off balance-sheet financing is a two-edged sword. While it may appear to be a superficial device which simply misleads the outside world about a company's true financial position at a given point in time, it can also be seen as a crucial provider of breathing-space. If a company does have genuinely short term financial problems which can be comfortably resolved in the fullness of time it is understandable that it would wish to deal with them in a tactful, subtle and unobtrusive fashion. The last thing it wants to do is create unjustified panic and undue concern which may lead to a loss of trust or credibility. Stability and confidence are important. Their value to a business cannot be underestimated, and, if off balance-sheet finance is the way to maintain such intangible assets, then so be it.

Leaving the moral issues aside for the time being, there is another difficulty with off balance-sheet financing and that is pinpointing the specific ways in which it is applied. There is an understandable conspiracy of silence between those who provide this form of financing and those who receive it. Both the givers and the takers have a lot to lose but even more to gain. The various schemes, therefore, go unpublicised, but it is possible to identify some which are in common use.

The starting-point for many schemes is the essential assets which a company needs to carry on its business. This is why leasing proved so popular and so successful a source of invisible finance. On the one hand the lessee needed the asset to allow the business to function and on the other, the lessor had guaranteed collateral, in that it retained the ultimate ownership of that asset. This is the basic principle which underpins the 'consignment stock' method of off balance-sheet finance.

The scheme is particularly appropriate for those businesses which effectively act as sales agents for a manufacturing company. The most obvious candidate is car dealerships. The manufacturer has a vested interest in selling vehicles, but knows full well that the only genuine sale is the one to the end user and not the mere delivery to the agent. The financing costs for the dealer of maintaining his stock of vehicles can be prohibitively high. Therefore, the consignment stock method of financing is brought into play.

Imagine the relationship between a car manufacturer and a dealer. Both share the same common interests but at the same time have to maintain their business dealings on a relatively commercial basis: enter the consignment stock approach to off balance-sheet financing. Under the scheme, stock is supplied by the manufacturer to the dealer on consignment. That is, no payment is made on delivery but only falls due when the stock is sold. Arrangements may vary, but a payment will only be made either immediately on sale or at some time shortly thereafter. However, although the manufacturer is clearly interested in ensuring that the dealer makes that crucial sale, it is not prepared to take the full brunt of the risks and financing of the stock without some recompense.

This might take the form of a deposit which the dealer is obliged to make to the manufacturer. More often than not it will be linked to the dealer's past record of vehicle sales. It is a reasonable arrangement since it eases the manufacturer's cash flow and, at the same time, provides a tangible incentive for the dealer to get on with the business of selling cars. Otherwise the manufacturer runs the risk of getting involved in what is little more than a very costly sale-or-return system of retailing. This deposit secures the dealer's right to obtain vehicles on consignment. However, the amounts of money will not be insignificant, and, for the dealer, will represent substantial liquid resources which are permanently tied up with the manufacturer. Clearly that deposit has to be financed and this is where the consignment scheme really begins to take effect.

Normally the deposit would be funded out of borrowings, which involves not just interest repayments, but may also divert funds from other parts of the business. Therefore, the manufacturer agrees to a scheme whereby it waives the deposit in return for a monthly waiver fee. This ensures that the car manufacturer retains an element of cash flow but, more importantly, it has great benefits for the dealer. The money which would have been permanently tied up in the deposit is immediately liberated. The waiver fee can be paid for out of the dealer's own cash flow which is much less of a burden.

In effect the manufacturer is financing the dealer's trading stock. However, that stock will not appear in the dealer's accounts and more importantly neither will the 'loan', which would otherwise have been necessary to ensure a constant supply of stock. The dealer is therefore free to seek further finance from its bank, should it so need, without the encumbrance of the deposit hanging over its shoulders.

Clearly there is an advantage in this arrangement for both parties. After all, the dealer and the manufacturer are working towards the same goal in that a sale of the car is the desired objective. The assumption is that the manufacturer has sufficient confidence in the dealer's operations to justify the financing it is effectively providing. The dangers with this form of off balance-sheet financing are more related to the distortions in the dealer's true position when it is dealing with its own bankers, or when it is being compared to another dealer which does not have the benefits of the same type of financing.

In the case above, the off balance-sheet financing is being provided almost as part of the normal working relationship between customer and supplier. It could be argued that this funding is a natural extension of that relationship and therefore acceptable, since it is little more than pragmatic commercial practice. The finance is not provided by way of hard cash, it simply frees funds which the dealer can then apply elsewhere in the business. However, the bulk of off balance-sheet financing arrangements bear little relationship to commercial reality. They are just ways of providing cash which will not appear anywhere in the company's accounts as borrowings.

Again, a business's stock and work in progress provide the ideal starting-point for such schemes. The 'artificial sale of stock' arrangement, as the name implies, relies heavily on the company's inventory for its success. It is particularly appropriate for businesses where the stock, or work in progress, must be retained for several years before it can be sold. A whisky distiller, or fine wine producer, might find the artificial sale method useful, since the products, especially those of the former, must be laid down for some time before they are ready for onward sale to the customer. The financing costs involved can be extremely heavy. It is not the simple storage costs which are the problem, but more the cash flow time-lag involved. The company incurs massive production costs in distilling the whisky, but then has to wait several years before these can be recovered when the cash received from its sale are received.

For well-established whisky producers there is a constant ebb and flow of some stocks being laid down and others being taken out on maturity for distribution and sale; this cash flow time-lag would be expected to have been absorbed in a production cycle which stretches back into the dim and distant past. This may well appear to be the case, but the fact remains that this financing cost of maturing stocks is always there and becomes much more pronounced when the business runs into temporary difficulties. The problems which have hit the British whisky industry are well rehearsed. Over-capacity has brought over-supply which has been translated into distress-selling of stocks on wafer-thin margins, or even at a loss, which has put the distillers under a lot of pressure.

Under these conditions it is easy to see why a company might want to resort to off balance-sheet financing. Traditional lines of credit may well be difficult to extend, since the banking community will be fully aware of the industry's problems and could therefore be reluctant to grant further borrowings to a business whose balance-sheet might already appear to have an uncomfortable level of gearing.

It puts the company in something of a Catch 22 situation since the borrowings might be needed not to finance the laying down of further stocks but rather to invest in new capital equipment which is needed to bring efficiencies to the production process. That investment may be essential if the company is to maintain its long term competitiveness and thus ensure its survival, but will be impossible to finance unless the banks take a relaxed and confident view of its prospects.

Enter the artificial sale of stock scheme. Under this arrangement the company sells its stock to a finance company. The credit for the disposal can be taken at that time but it is not a genuine sale, since the company will retain an option to repurchase the stock at a future date. It is an option which it will most certainly want to exercise. After all, the finance company is in the business of finance and the distilling company is in the business of distilling. The sale is clearly artificial since while the stock is blissfully unaware that its owner is now somebody completely different, it will not usually leave the company's premises and will happily get on with the business of maturing.

The repurchase price will of course be higher than the original selling price. It will normally be based on the market price at the time of resale, on the assumption that this has been rising, or on the original sales price adjusted upwards for the rolled up interest which has accrued during the period of ownership. So, when the whisky has matured and is ready for consumption by the eager consumer, the buy back option is exercised, the finance house is repaid and life continues as if nothing untoward had happened.

The difference between the original price at which the stock was sold to the finance house and the price at which it is repurchased is, in effect, a financing charge which replaces the interest that the company would have had to pay had it been funding the stock, while it matured, out of externally generated borrowings. The financing charge is, however, likely to be higher than that incurred using commercial interest rates.

The impact on the finances of the distilling company as a consequence of this transaction is considerable. Firstly it could, if it so wished, bring the sale of the stocks forward to the time when the deal with the finance house is struck. It is not an option which would be favoured unless the sales position of the company looked distinctly unflattering at the time of the deal. More likely, the sale would be accounted for once it was sold on to a *bona fide* customer. This way the company would not have to bear the cost of the full repurchase price; it would simply take the difference between the original selling price and the buy-back price, the financing element of the deal, and classify it as a cost of sale in the year when the stock is repurchased.

Second, and more important for the company, it has the free use of the funds raised throughout the artificial sale of the stock for the duration of the whisky's maturity period. The funds can be applied in whatever direction the company wishes, either to meet short term cash flow shortfalls or to finance crucial investment projects. Whatever the reasons for needing to use the scheme, the effect is still the same, the loan does not appear in the balance-sheet. Neither does the stock which has been sold. This may well be important if the company wants to demonstrate that it does not have a big stockholding problem.

In this respect, the scheme is similar to the consignment stock approach to off balance-sheet finance, in that neither the loan nor the assets to which it directly relates appear in the company's accounts.

Still on the theme of using current assets to secure financing which does not have to be disclosed on the balance-sheet as a loan, is the 'assignment of work in progress' scheme. This time, rather than an asset and the corresponding liability simply being excluded from the accounts, the arrangement results in a reduction of the value which is attributed to the company's work in progress. It is a method of off balance-sheet financing which is naturally most appropriate for those businesses which have long term contracts which take some years to complete. The construction companies spring immediately to mind as potential users of this kind of scheme. Again the underlying reasons for adopting the scheme will be those related to short term cash flow shortages and already high gearing ratios.

Like the distillers which have to finance stock for several years before they can realise the investment which it ties up, the construction companies are also faced with the difficulty of financing a long term project which will only produce cash some time after the necessary costs have been incurred. Again the spread of contracts and the timing of their completion would normally be expected to smooth out this lag in cash flow receipts. However, the construction industry has also found itself in difficulties on an international and national basis. The margins to be earned are barely noticeable and with competition intense, to say the least, the initiative remains very much with the giver of contract rather than the receiver. Front-end start-up costs are considerable, and these have to be financed at a time when the banks remain dubious about increasing the levels of lending.

A further problem for the construction companies lies with the regular difficulties, which they face during highly competitive times, in obtaining progress payments on the contract. International contracts for developing companies tend to be the most problematic, with a combination of administrative bureaucracy and balance of payments difficulties often leading to a delay in the cash being passed on to the construction company. It is to counter these cash flow irregularities, and at the same time keep the balance sheet gearing in check, that a company will adopt the assignment of work in progress approach to counter the problem.

The company will again deal through a bank or finance house. It agrees to assign irrevocably all the amounts which are payable under a major contract to the financier. At the same time the company also issues a bond which guarantees the performance of the contract, which ensures that it is legally bound to complete the work. Having secured the assignment and the performance bond, the finance house will then make periodic cash advances to the company. This will normally be in advance of work being carried out and allows the company to purchase the necessary materials and meet the other essential costs relating to the contract. Having made these advances the finance house also charges interest at a rate which will have been agreed as part of the deal.

This allows the construction company to carry out the contract without undue worry about the timing of progress payments from the client and without putting pressure on its other cash flow projections and the underlying strength, or weakness, of the balance sheet.

The scheme is devised in such a way that once the construction company has repaid the full amount of the cash advances, together with any interest which has accrued, the balance outstanding under the contract is reassigned by the bank to the company. The arrangement therefore has considerable flexibility since the company can control the rate at which the advances are repaid. This might be at the same pace as the receipt of progress payments from the client or, if cash flow elsewhere in the business permits, at a quicker rate.

At the same time, the terms of the assignment contract and the nature of the performance bond ensure that the company has no direct obligation to repay to the bank the amounts which it has advanced in order to finance the project. This means that there is no need for the company to disclose the advances in its accounts as a loan, and the borrowing remains well and truly off balance sheet. The advances are treated simply as a reduction in the value of the company's work in progress, in the same way that normal progress payments on account would be disclosed.

However, the transaction does not have complete immunity from disclosure requirements. The nature and terms of the performance bond dictate that a contingent liability is created, and its existence must therefore be disclosed in the company's accounts by way of a note. That note can be vaguely drafted in such a way as not to reveal the full impact of the bond on the accounts and the company's off balance-sheet financing activities, which allow it to reduce reported borrowings, remain a closely guarded secret.

All three schemes which have so far been examined have

been directly related to the company's assets. In many cases, the underlying reason for using these off balance-sheet financing methods will be simply to fund the assets to which the schemes relate. The common theme to all three schemes is that not only do the borrowings not appear in the balance sheet but neither do the assets, be they stock or work in progress.

It could therefore be argued that such schemes are merely practical solutions to commercial problems. Shareholders and users of accounts are not being deceived, since the missing liability is matched by the missing asset. This argument does not, however, hold water when the funds are being raised to finance other projects, or when commercial prudence would have dictated that the funds would not have been made available under straightforward borrowing arrangements. There is no doubt that off balance-sheet financing, in whatever form, distorts the true state of a company's borrowings, which not only impairs comparability with other businesses, but might also lead to misinformed business or investment decisions being taken by those who are obliged to rely on the accounts.

However, it must still be said that the schemes so far reviewed do have the feature, not in itself redeeming, of being linked to some real commercial aspect of the business. In this respect they differ wildly from the two remaining schemes, analysed below, which are totally detached from any genuine transaction. These are little more than artificial devices to raise cash for the business without informing the outside world.

The simpler of the two is the 'redeemable preference share' scheme. This is, in effect, a method which allows borrowings to be classified as part of the company's share capital. It is a scheme which will be used not by the main holding company but rather by one of its subsidiaries. This subsidiary simply issues redeemable preference shares with a dividend which equates to current interest rates. Those preference shares are then taken up by a bank or finance house.

The subsidiary is happy with the arrangement since it is then free to use the cash as it wishes. This may be transferred throughout the group to finance projects or investments as the need arises. The bank is also happy, since it will be receiving dividends which compensate it for the interest it has foregone on the cash issued to the company in order to purchase the preference shares.

The biggest winner, though, is the holding company itself. For while the subsidiary is obliged to disclose the preference shares in its own balance-sheet, its accounts are rarely scrutinised by the public. The main focus of attention is on the holding company's accounts, and here the preference shares are shown in the group's balance-sheet as little more than a minority interest. It is impossible to detect from this the loan element of the transaction. Yet the group still has the use of the money which has been raised without, in any way, reflecting this in its own reported borrowings. By using the subsidiary as the medium for raising the finance, those funds are allowed to remain unnoticed off the group's own balance-sheet.

This principle is extended in the final, and by far the most sinister, method of off balance-sheet financing. This is the non-disclosed subsidiary scheme. As the name suggests, it goes much further than merely using a subsidiary company for off balance-sheet fund-raising. Instead, a company is formed which has the attributes of a subsidiary in everything other than strict legal interpretation. It is another example of the continuing conflict between the practical substance of a transaction and its legal form.

The company is formed by issuing its share capital in such a way that it is not, under the strictest legal interpretation, a subsidiary as defined and laid down by section 154 of the 1948 Companies Act. This is not the end of the story. The subsidiary's legal and capital structure can be constructed so that the holding company does not just get the benefit of a subsidiary which does not have to be treated as such in its accounts. Additionally it can classify the offshoot as a subsidiary for tax purposes so that it can take full advantage of the group taxation relief provisions. This curious and apparently ludicrous position arises because of the different rules which apply when deciding what is a subsidiary for accounts disclosure purposes and what is a subsidiary for taxation purposes.

The holding company, therefore, not only gets its off balance-sheet financing cake, but also gets to eat it.

There are several ways of constructing this invisible subsidiary all of which are, by their very nature, quite complex. They are, however, with a little help from a company's financial advisers, surprisingly easy to implement.

Perhaps the most simple example of the non-disclosed subsidiary is that which involves a share capital combining both ordinary shares and those described as 'A' preference shares. Under company legislation in this country both types of share are classified as equity capital, which is, of course, important for ensuring that the subsidiary will ultimately remain off balance-sheet. The ordinary and 'A' preference shares are issued in equal numbers. In order to make the scheme work, the holding company takes into its ownership, the ordinary shares which are issued. The parent's bankers then take up the 'A' preference shares.

However, the nature of corporate legislation relating to disclosure dictates that the rules relating to the composition of the board of directors of the new company must also be considered. Equal holding of the offshoot's share capital is insufficient to ensure that it will escape disclosure. Company law recognises that composition of the board of directors is equally important in deciding true ownership of a business. Therefore, in setting up the subsidiary, its articles are constructed in such a way to ensure that the holding company and the bank have the right to appoint an equal number of directors.

This equality of board composition could pose some practical problems for the parent company because it is deprived of physical control of the directors. There are two ways round this difficulty, neither of which preclude the ultimate objective of creating a subsidiary whose activities are not required to be disclosed and treated in the accounts as such.

The first balance-sheet by-pass is for the parent not just to hold the ordinary shares but also to hold some loan stock in the subsidiary. That loan stock carries with it the right for the parent to a further director to the board and this, in effect, secures voting control of the board. Alternatively, the articles which set out the rules for appointing the directors could allocate two votes to those appointed by holders of ordinary shares, the equity held by the parent, and just one vote to the directors appointed by holders of the 'A' preference shares, which are held by the bank. Neither method will impinge on the decision on whether or not the newly-formed company is classed as a subsidiary.

That decision rests on the answer to two simple questions. Does the holding company own more than 50 per cent of the equity share capital, and does it control composition of the board of directors? If either question is answered in the affirmative, the new company must be deemed to be a subsidiary; it must be accounted for and disclosed as such in the group financial statements. Clearly, though, by using the method outline above, the answer to both questions is negative. The equity share capital of the new company, even though it comprises two different types of shares, is held equally by the parent and by the bank. The law makes no distinction between the different classes and looks simply at the totality of the issued share capital. More important is the percentage which is held. The crucial words here are 'more than': as long as the parent holds up to and including 50 per cent it passes the test and can say with hand on heart that the answer to the question on share ownership is 'no'.

Similarly, on the question about the board of directors, the parent can give the same answer: the key word here is 'composition'. This is something totally different from control. For although the parent will ensure that its representatives have the majority of votes on the board, it does not actually have control of the physical composition. It is the articles which determine how the board is made up, since it sets out the numbers which can be appointed by each class of shareholder. The fact that the votes attaching to those directors may differ is neither here nor there in the context of 'composition'. Even if the parent has chosen the loan stock route to appoint an additional director with a casting vote, the answer to the question on board composition can still be answered in the negative. This is because the right given to the holder of the loan stock to make that appointment is not itself a right which is available as a consequence of owning equity capital of the new company. Care must be taken, however, where the parent also holds ordinary shares. The loan stock director is therefore ignored for the purposes of the composition test, and once again the parent can truthfully give the answer 'no'.

This double negative leaves the parent with a highly important asset in that it now has a company over which it has boardroom control but which, according to the relevant legislation, is not technically a subsidiary. The method set out above is not the only way of achieving this version of corporate Utopia. There are endless variations on the same theme which use different combinations of equity capital, complex cross-shareholding by different group companies, and a subtle blend of directorial appointments to get the desired result. Irrespective of the means, the parent company always achieves the same devastating end.

Having created this subsidiary, which is not a subsidiary, the parent company is then free to sit back and take advantage of it as and when it sees fit. The main benefit is that since the new company is not legally a subsidiary there is no requirement for it to be consolidated and incorporated in the group balance-sheet. Its assets and liabilities, which would normally have been reflected in the holding company's financial affairs, are ignored completely. True, the new company will have to be recognised as an associated or related company, but this will not have any substantial effect on the group position since this will simply result in the holding company accounting for the relevant share of the new company's results.

The real strength, then, on the non-disclosed subsidiary is the scope it offers for raising finance which does not have to be shown in the parent's accounts. Any borrowings would be almost impossible to identify, and it becomes possible for the holding company to raise cash at will, while still giving the impression of being either lowly geared or at least fully in control of a balance-sheet which is already highly geared.

The ways of raising the finance through the company are

legion. It is not simply a question of borrowing large sums of money and then distributing them throughout the group to meet the various cash requirements. This is certainly a possibility, but adopting this approach may result in the funds given to other group subsidiaries showing up in their accounts as loans, which might then have to be reflected in the holding company's accounts.

There might be some scope for netting these off as intra-group loans, but as the new company will not be consolidated this may well be limited. Further, the fledgeling company will have no assets of its own to speak of, and bankers may well be reluctant to advance it loans without some element of security. Better, then, to use some other method of spreading the off balance-sheet finance throughout the group. The parent or another legitimate subsidiary might, for instance, sell some of its assets to the invisible subsidiary and use these as collateral for a loan. The word 'sell' is used in the loosest possible sense of the word, since the sales agreement may well contain a buy-back clause which gives the vendor an option to repurchase the assets at some later date at the same price. It is an option which will doubtless be exercised at a time which is convenient to the group's financial affairs.

A second approach might be for the group company to sell its debtors to the new company which, in turn, sells them on at a discount to the bank. This achieves the same effect as the previous method, bringing the cash cleanly into the group structure. Legitimate fixed or current assets are thus being replaced with legitimate cash, but in a thoroughly artificial manner.

That artificiality is not, however, illegal. The transactions involved, while not necessarily being above board, are certainly not below it. However, the nature of these arrangements, and their very existence, must be a cause for concern. They are in grave danger of becoming the unacceptable face of creative accounting.

The main problem with off balance-sheet financing in general, and with the non-disclosable subsidiary method in particular, is that it threatens to distort the truth and fairness of the accounts. While there is no legal requirement for companies to report these schemes in their accounts, the chances of creative accounting becoming deceptive accounting are greatly increased. Contrast the approach in this country with that in the United States where, until recently, there has been no requirement for companies to consolidate the debt of its controlled subsidiaries. This strange practice will shortly be brought to an end. The main point, though, is that while the consolidation was not required, details of the amounts involved still had to be published in the accounts. Thus the user of the financial statements, providing he read the accounts properly, was not misled, and could draw his own conclusions about the group's total debt position. In Britain, while we may have to consolidate the debt of subsidiaries, there is no requirement to publish any information about off balance-sheet financing.

Shareholders and other users of the accounts are therefore making decisions under a cloud of uncertainty, using information which may be neither full nor fair. A group which, according to its published balance-sheet, may have little or no borrowings, could in fact be riddled with debt which has been arranged off balance-sheet. The great problem is that there is no way of telling which companies have used such schemes. Even the group's auditors might struggle, because of the nature of the beast, to identify the existence of such arrangements, and will thus be unable to assess whether they affect the account's truth and fairness.

There is an increasing awareness within the accountancy profession that the problem cannot go untackled for too much longer. The excellent pioneering work carried out by Professor David Tweedie of accountants KMG Thomson McLintock, on which this chapter draws heavily, has prompted swift action, and his concern has also been echoed by the regulatory financial authorities such as the Bank of England. The upshot of Professor Tweedie's prompting should be that off balance-sheet financing is relegated to the same shady category as the now discredited window-dressing, which was perhaps the forefather of the current schemes.

The different perceptions of window-dressing and off

balance-sheet finance is reflected in their names. The former sounds shabby and deceitful while the latter sounds honourable and effective. However, the effect of both is to misrepresent and mislead, and the only questions are to what extent and for what purpose?

The true colours of window-dressing were spelt out to great effect in a Department of Trade report into the Cornhill Consolidated Group, the collapsed investment bank. The report said: 'A balance sheet describes the state of affairs existing at a particular point in time. Although a true and fair view may be given of a company's state of affairs at the end of its financial year, this may not be representative of its state of affairs at any other time. A company's capital, reserves and liabilities, and consequently its assets, may change swiftly and dramatically in the course of its business.'

Having described the nature of the balance-sheet and its propensity to change, the report then points out: 'Such a change may, however, be deliberately contrived with the primary purpose of improving the appearance of a company given by its balance-sheet. This practice is generally known as "window-dressing". This, however, is a euphemism: the purpose of window-dressing is deception.'

It is a clear exposition of the unsavoury nature of that practice, but it also highlights some similarities with off balance-sheet financing, the purpose of some of the schemes which are available being clearly intended to show the company's position in a more favourable light.

However, the report also highlights some of the difficulties in pinning down these arrangements. It concedes that, because the balance-sheet has to give a true and fair view at a particular point in time and at no other, it is hard to determine how window-dressing carried out before that point affects the truth and fairness of this part of the accounts. The report states: 'Balance-sheet window-dressing in the Cornhill Group, though contrived, was achieved by means of actual transactions with third parties prior to the end of the financial year.'

Once again there are parallels with off balance-sheet financing, which is certainly contrived but also relies on actual transactions with third parties. The chances, therefore, of such schemes distorting, on a purely technical and legalistic basis, the truth and fairness of the balance-sheet at its year end, and on that day alone, must be somewhat limited.

However, such conditions did not deter the inspectors who wrote the report on Cornhill Consolidated Group. Referring to reciprocal loan arrangements, under which a loan from a third party was passed through two or more groups or related companies in repayment of existing indebtedness, and then back on loan to a third party, they said: 'A balance-sheet which reflects one side of a reciprocal loan arrangement may give a true and fair view, but in our opinion it can only do so if full disclosure is made of both the nature of the reciprocal arrangements and their effect on the disposition of the company's assets and liabilities.'

Few would disagree with this and, given the clear similarities between window-dressing and off balance-sheet financing, there must be a strong case for approaching the young pretender to the creative accounting throne in a similar fashion. The arguments for, if not the outlawing off balance-sheet financing, certainly improving the disclosure requirements, are compelling.

The complex nature of the transactions and the way in which they are implemented may make control difficult, but this is not a reason in itself to ignore the problem. The underlying reason for off balance-sheet financing is to present the company's financial position in a different and more favourable light. This is at best unsatisfactory and at worst unsavoury, and the reporting régime which allows these arrangements to fester and to prosper must therefore be changed as a matter of some urgency.

The Cornhill Insurance Group inspectors encapsulated the current problem when they said: 'In our view such arrangements, since they are designed to deceive, should not be condoned either by directors of companies or by their auditors. The practice of balance sheet window-dressing would seem to have gained partial acceptance by many professional accountants, who seem to regard themselves as unable to discourage such arrangements unless they are carried out to such a material extent that the auditors are of the opinion that the accounts do not give a true and fair view of the company's state of affairs. We believe that this situation could be substantially improved if the accountants' professional bodies were to issue guidance on this subject to their members.'

Guidance from the accountancy profession is probably the only practical way of dealing with the off balance-sheet financing problem. There is little prospect of the government coming to the rescue by introducing changes in company legislation because of the principle that any emphasis on substance over form must not be at the expense of compliance with the law. If this avenue is blocked then the only way forward must be through improved disclosure, justified by the overriding requirement for accounts to show a true and fair view. Linked with a clearer appreciation within the auditing profession of the nature and general principles of off balance-sheet financing schemes, and a better understanding of the tell-tale signs which indicate their presence in an organisation, there is a real chance that the cancer can be gouged out of corporate balance-sheets before it has the opportunity to spread.

Until this is done, and done effectively, off balance-sheet financing will continue to threaten the relevance and reliability of company accounts. And while the schemes are actively marketed by the merchant banks they will be given an air of acceptability which is totally unwarranted. The arguments to justify off balance-sheet financing are similar to those used to support the publishing and sale of pornography, in that it fulfils a genuine corporate need and therefore is a service to society. To legislate against it would only drive it underground and make it even more difficult to control.

There may well be some substance to this but, like pornography, the reasons for its existence do nothing to make it more palatable.

It must be said, however, that these schemes are extremely effective tools for a corporate management which wants to disguise its true financial position to a greater or lesser extent. Be it to smooth out short term cash flow fluctuations or to create the illusion of a sounder financial stability, off balance-sheet financing does work.

For shareholders and users of accounts there is little protection from the distortions which can be created. All they can do is read financial statements extremely carefully, paying particular attention to changes in the group structure, details of contingent liabilities and to unusual fluctuations in the group borrowings position. After that, the best thing to do is to cross all fingers, legs and toes and hope for the best.

15

HOW CREATIVE ACCOUNTING is used in the OIL INDUSTRY

Convincing evidence of the widespread nature of creative accounting comes from an analysis of the accounts of companies in the oil and gas sector. The 1985 edition of accountants Peat Marwick's 'UK Accounting Principles and Presentation: Oil and Gas' provides a clear indication that the sector is riddled with manipulation and, although it does not quantify the financial impact, it highlights the wide variety of accounting treatments and presentation which are the meat and drink of the creative accountant.

The oil sector is unusual in that it comprises a whole range of companies, ranging from the well-established majors such as Shell and BP right down to the smallest exploration enterprises. Those companies all offer their unique risks and rewards yet they all have one thing in common; their statutory accounts rarely provide the information which investors need to make a rational and well-informed assessment of the real prospects.

City analysts openly admit that they pay little, if any, attention to the annual report and accounts. These are regarded as being worse then useless since they contain no information about the all-important reserves which determine the oil or gas company's future prospects. Instead the analysts rely on their own extensive knowledge of the industry, which derives from a continuous and careful study of the sector and the external factors which affect it. Unfortunately that acquired intelligence is not available to the small private investors who have to rely on the report and accounts for the bulk of their financial information. Their needs are much greater than those of the specialist investment analyst who looks at the accounts only, for a broad guide to the company's corporate philosophy rather than a specific indication of its actual worth. So, while the experts play around with their cash flow projections and esti-mates of proven reserves, the private investor is left with the financial statements to provide some comfort and solace. The survey from Peat Marwick, however, shows there is little actually on offer from this particular source. To start with, from the 44 companies in the survey there are three different types of profit and loss account and three different types of balance-sheet formats on offer. From this starting-point of disagreement the position gradually deteriorates.

There are, for example, tremendous discrepancies in the attitude to disclosure of accounting policies and these are pretty important in assessing how a company has approached the preparation of the figures which appear in the accounts. Yet there were only 3 accounting policies which all 44 companies felt warranted some attention; well over 20 other policies remained which some companies felt should be disclosed while others saw no need to do so.

One of the few policies which all companies disclosed was that on depletion, depreciation and amortisation. Yet even here there was absolutely no consistency of treatment. A total of 11 differently worded accounting policies were recorded. Some of the policies might have meant exactly the same thing, but this is not immediately apparent to the uninitiated. The same trend appears consistently throughout the various sets of accounts: there is simply no single treatment which is common to all the companies. Within those variations the creative accountant finds the perfect environment for working his craft.

As if this were not enough, there is worse to follow for the poor private investor who has to rely on published financial statements for his information. Not only is there inconsistency between the companies within the sector, there is also incon-sistency within individual companies year on year. There were no fewer than 14 changes of accounting policy reported, which was actually an increase in percentage terms on the previous year. This means that around one third of all the companies in the sector played around with their accounting policies, thus allowing them the chance for some creative accounting in the process.

It is perhaps not a coincidence that the policies which seem most prone to change, or where there is the greatest variance, are those which have already featured in the chapters of this book. Stock valuation, which has already been demonstrated as a highly sensitive and important figure, threw up 6 different methods among the 22 companies which had oil and gas stocks at the year end. These included the lower of average cost of net realisable value, the lower of FIFO cost or net realisable value, production cost and market value. However, a disturbing 4 companies gave no indication of the method of valuation which had been used, so making it impossible, of course, for an investor to make any sense of how the company has approached this delicate subject.

On turnover, which is again an area where a company can manipulate its income quite substantially, there were once again 6 different policies on display. This excludes 4 other accounting policies, which had been used by companies in the previous year, but which had disappeared from the 1985 survey. The policies ranged from a simple invoiced sales approach to the more subjective accruals basis. Once again there were 6 companies which did not bother to disclose a policy, while a further 4 did not disclose any turnover at all.

The oil and gas sector was not slow either to take advantage of the vague rules on exceptional and extraordinary items: 25 companies incurred costs or, in rare circumstances, received income then classified as extraordinary. These included closure cost provisions, disposals of fixed assets, and operations and provisions against the value of investments. There was, of course, some clear disagreement over the interpretation of the rules. Industrial Scotland Energy, for instance, deemed that the costs of a rights issue was extraordinary, while Highland Participants treated the expenses of its rights issue as exceptional. There was also some disagreement on whether write-offs against the value of investments should be taken above or below the line. Both schools of thought found supporters. Again this makes it difficult for investors to make any reasoned comparison between the performances of companies in the sector.

Perhaps the most disturbing weakness in the accounts of oil and gas companies is the lack of information on reserves. This, you might think, would be crucial for any meaningful understanding of the financial statements, since the oil and gas reserves represent the lifeblood of the business. However, there is no mandatory requirement for a company to disclose any reserve or production data in its accounts. Instead investors have to rely on their own intuition, be it well-researched, in the case of the specialist analyst, or purely speculative, in the case of the private investor.

Even without a mandatory requirement, some 14 companies did give some limited information, in a variety of guises ranging from the notes to the accounts to a reproduction of an independent valuation report, of oil and gas reserves. Although it still must be better than nothing at all the extent that the information varied may cause the cynics to wonder why the company was going to the trouble of producing such detailed non-statutory information. However, this still leaves 30 companies which gave no information at all about the state of their crucial oil and gas reserves, leaving some shareholders with little more than guesswork on which to base their investment decisions.

In spite of all these differences, though, all the companies received audit reports which said that the accounts, even for the seven companies which received a qualified opinion, showed a true and fair view. Whether this is an indictment of the wording of the report is not really the question. The fact is that 44 companies in the same sector can produce information relating to similar activities on completely different bases, with widely varying levels of disclosure and still receive a seal of approval from their auditors at the end of the day.

Creative accounting is alive and well and thriving in not just the oil sector but in every walk of corporate life. To ignore it, either as a manager or shareholder, would be churlish.

16

WHY you shouldn't believe EVERYTHING YOU READ

Whether the differences in accounting treatment and presentation are real or imagined, it is clear that there is scope for tremendous variation in reported figures. But is there any way in which this can be improved? The answer is probably not. The system of accounting standards was set in motion in January 1970 in response to the very accusation that there was no framework to govern how companies should prepare their accounts. By and large, the individual standards have not changed substantially since they were first introduced. There have been some refinements in response to changes in tax and company law, but the main thrust of the standards has remained unchanged.

It is pertinent that the review of the standard setting process carried out by the ASC in October 1982 concluded that the process was in need of review and was capable of improvement. However, that improvement was to be achieved, not by more standards, but by less. These would deal only with matters of major and fundamental importance affecting the generality of companies. Rather than on increased prescriptive powers the emphasis was instead to be on better and more effective consultation and communication. The review also introduced several layers into the standard setting process which allowed for statements of intent and statements of recommended practice that do not have any mandatory status. But the most important conclusion was that the

ASC would stick with its traditional stance of not issuing interpretations of accounting standards. This failure to grasp the opportunity to take a more active role in this crucial area might still prove to have been an oversight.

There is a growing feeling in certain quarters of the ASC that it needs greater enforcement powers if it to is be an effective arbiter and setter of the best accounting practice. That lobby has not been helped by the ASC's official stance of non-intervention on the interpretation of contentious issues. By shying away from that responsibility, the auditor is left as the main instrument of enforcement. However, he is constrained by the individual and unique pressures which are a direct consequence of a close working relationship with his client. This can sometimes cloud and influence the auditor's judgement and might also lead to different interpretations by different firms. The differences in acceptable accounting treatments on specific areas are therefore not only endorsed but also perpetuated.

For the time being, then, there is no immediate sign that the ASC will be given the teeth that it needs to enforce stricter compliance with its standards. That would require not just a change in attitude on the part of the ASC, in accepting greater responsibility for interpretation and enforcement, but also an acceptance of government intervention by the accountancy profession at large. Any system which embodied greater enforcement powers would inevitably require the backing of law. Yet the accountancy profession has always resisted government intervention, preferring to maintain that self-regulation is the way forward. This may well be the case as far as the internal machinations of the profession are concerned, but it cannot apply to accounting standards where the enforcement has to be imposed on corporate managements, which are not generally members of the main accountancy bodies.

In fact the ASC has already admitted that it does need government support in some areas, by its request for statutory backing for an inflation accounting standard. Such legislative support for a single accounting standard would not in itself achieve very much: it is more an acceptance of defeat than an attempt to make a positive step forward in the standards enforcement arena. If any progress is to be made on this front, a fully-fledged, properly funded government-backed enforcement agency, akin to the Securities and Exchange Commission which operates in the USA, is called for. Only such a technically competent and independent body, supported by statutory backing, will have any chance of improving strict compliance with accounting standards.

But the accountancy profession is not the only obstacle to such an innovation. The accounts preparers in industry and commerce might well put up stout resistance to such a move. Finance directors have become attached to the flexibility permitted by the current legal and accounting régime. And as long as there are no embarrassing incidents, where it can be shown that an abuse of creative accounting has resulted directly in huge financial losses being incurred by the general public, there would appear to be little to support the argument that the present system of flexibility is inappropriate. It would require an organisation like British Telecom to go bust as a consequence of excessive creative accounting before people would sit up and listen to suggestions that something had to be done. Until that unlikely event occurs there is little prospect of any improvement in the current system being generated by way of reaction to abuses of creative accounting by corporate managements.

Perhaps some pressure for reform may come from the Take-over Panel. The recent outbreak of merger mania and the increasing use of creative accounting in fighting take-over battles might produce some fall-out. There is a limit to the number and extent of profit forecasts which can be made purely on the back of creative accounting techniques. If the various bids and deals result in excessive abuse of financial information, the Take-over Panel may be forced to call for a termination of hostilities, and insist on a return to some kind of accounting order. However, the influence of creative accounting on take-over tactics is not new, and there have been enough examples of its misuse already to have inspired a clamp-down if this had been needed.

Another source of pressure for change might be the state of the stock market itself. While it has been in an upward surging bull phase, investors have not had too much to worry about. Capital growth and dividend payments have been readily available for all. But if the bear market takes a grip it may be a different story. Companies may find it difficult to cope with the demands of a plummeting market, and some of the creative accounting sins may find their perpetrators out. However, as long as the bear market did not result in widespread financial collapse, and assuming that the underlying trading position of most companies was unaffected, this may still not be a sufficient incentive to bring about substantial changes in the financial accounting and reporting régime. However, when people start losing money in large quantities then questions begin to be asked with a little more urgency.

Perhaps the creative accounting techniques which are most likely to result in financial losses for outside investors and creditors in large quantities are the off balance-sheet financing schemes. Their dangers, and the difficulties in quantifying and identifying them, have already been explored elsewhere. Unless positive moves are made to ensure that the existence of such schemes and their financial implications are clearly identified in the accounts, there is a real danger that they will cause untold damage to the credibility of financial statements. This may well require the government to rethink its stance on the argument over whether the practical substance or legal form of a transaction should take precedence. Without some changes in company legislation at least to recognise the existence and dangers of off balance-sheet financing, an entire corporate finance black market may spring up. It is a daunting prospect, but, providing action is taken on these schemes and taken swiftly and effectively, they are unlikely to undermine the effectiveness of the more traditional creative accounting methods.

But if these external factors do not provide the incentive for some kind of reform of the existing reporting and disclosure requirements, is there anything that those more closely connected with them can do to bring about change? The auditor is after all appointed, in theory, by the shareholders, to protect their interests, so can some initiatives be expected on this front? The answer is likely to be in the negative, at least while the auditor is operating in the vacuum created by the vagueness of the true and fair view.

Unless the government provides a much more specific and tighter definition of what is meant by a true and fair view, it will be impossible for auditors to take any widespread action against misused creative accounting. Many would not want to do so anyway. However, their cause would be helped by clearer and firmer interpretations of accounting standards, and this might provide the encouragement needed by auditors to take a firmer stance against the more dubious creative accounting practices. That stance may be inspired anyway by the increase in negligence claims brought against auditors over their work on clients which subsequently went bust. The increase in the level and number of those claims, and the difficulty the firms have had in securing indemnity insurance to protect them from such claims, has resulted in many firms looking more closely at audit risk, that is the chances of a client running into financial difficulties. While the question of the auditor's unlimited liability remains unresolved, there is a clear incentive for the firms to resist creative accounting practices which might ultimately backfire and pose problems, not just for the company but indirectly for the auditors as well.

Such closer attention to the problem may bring some improvements but, given the subjective nature of the judgements which are linked with creative accounting it may be difficult for any substantial inroads to be made. In the end it is the company's management which has the responsibility for preparing and presenting the financial statements so it is perhaps to them that we should look for self-imposed improvements in the current system.

To suggest that they should all desist from all creative accounting activities forthwith would be both improper and impractical. There is no doubt that companies do need to retain some element of flexibility over their accounting. However, that flexibility must be tempered by a large element of realism, which should ensure that there is no abuse of the opportunities available. These are provided to encourage a fairer disclosure of results, not their distortion. Creative accounting can certainly, if used prudently and properly, assist in a better understanding of the financial performance from a company. However, as with so many things, there always seems to be a mindless minority which is determined to spoil it for everybody. It is these less discerning accounting conjurers who pose the greatest cause for concern, and provide the evidence that the subject cannot be quietly ignored and left on one side.

It is unlikely that these cowboys will inspire the government to legislate against them. However, there are certain areas where an improvement in company law would help. In particular, greater emphasis should be placed on the nature and level of disclosure requirements. As long as a company spells out exactly what it has done, and quantifies the financial effect of various accounting treatments, the shareholder has the information which is necessary to make an informed assessment of the company's performance, and should be able to draw valid comparisons with other companies. However, for this theory to work in practice, it is necessary for all companies to attain similar levels of disclosure. It is no good relying on individual management to undertake this of their own volition, and, in the end, legislation will be needed.

One area where big improvements could be made is on the disclosure of accounting policies. Too often they are virtually useless. The phraseology is either too vague or too technical, and it is almost impossible to determine exactly what bases and assumptions a company has been using in preparing its accounts. A clearer and more accurate description of accounting policies would be a very positive step in the direction of improved understanding. Greater emphasis should also be placed on the statement of sources and applications of fund statement. It is the closest that a company comes to preparing an analysis of its cash flow. Too many businesses treat it as a necessary evil, yet, if properly constructed, it could give a very informed insight into the progress of the enterprise. It would throw up any glaring discrepancies between reported profits and cash flows, which might give an indication of the extent of any creative accounting which has been used.

However, the chances of government intervention to improve disclosure in financial statements is perhaps remote. This is not a reflection of a lack of incentive or opportunity. Given the attention which has been paid to protecting investors, and clamping down on corporate fraud, the climate would appear ripe for improvement. The government has acknowledged that some changes need to be made in order to clarify the nature of the accounting records which a company needs to maintain; also that greater emphasis has to be placed on the management's duty to ensure that there are adequate controls of those records and over the company's assets, which will allow it to safeguard the shareholder's investment.

On the premise that the distinction between creative accounting and fraud is only thinly drawn, it should follow that the government has a vested interest in ensuring that the distinction is more clearly identified. It would be a shame if it missed its opportunity to make some improvements in the current régime in the name of investor protection and fraud prevention.

Given that the chances of the various third parties coming to the aid of the shareholder are somewhat remote, it would be unwise for the investing community to rely on this intervention to safeguard its interests. In the final analysis the old adage of 'let the buyer beware' must continue to hold true. The most reliable protection for the shareholder may still prove to be his own investigations and analysis of the company's performance. For all the shortcomings of a set of accounts there is still a tremendous amount of information on view. Close and careful scrutiny of that information may in the long run yield dividends which are more valuable than the hard cash which the company pays out each year. Some simple comparisons between the format and presentation of the financial statements year on year will be useful, and a record of key performance ratios might be kept. It may appear like a lot of hard work but, when the odds are stacked so heavily against you, you need all the help you can get. Similarly, the shareholder should be fully aware of the right of access to information about the company's affairs which he has. The opportunity to scrutinise such records should not be missed, and, if possible, the annual general meeting should be attended, so that the company's officers can be questioned more closely on the accounts.

But perhaps the best safeguard is to look upon the annual accounts with a more cynical and jaundiced eye. The myth that the financial statements are an irrefutable and accurate reflection of the company's trading performance for the year must be exploded once and for all. The accounts are little more than an indication of a broad trend. They include a built-in margin for error of a least ten per cent, and have been subject to all kinds of massage and manipulation. As a stand-alone document of record they have limited value.

If the shareholder is fully aware of these shortcomings, and, at the same time, fully appreciates the motives for a company to indulge in creative accounting, he is better placed to take a more considered overview of the past performance and future prospects. Once the psychological barrier which prevents shareholders from mistrusting the company's accounts is broken down, they will be able to adopt a healthy and questioning disregard for the information which they contain.

Blessed is the shareholder who expects nothing from a set of accounts for he shall not be disappointed.

THE CHANGE MASTERS: *Corporate Entrepreneurs at Work*
Rosabeth Moss Kanter

The Change Masters vividly demonstrates that when environ-
ments and structures are hospitable to innovation, people's
natural inventiveness and power skills can make almost
anything happen. Professor Kanter's fascinating book is an
indispensable guide for individuals who seek to realise their
entrepreneurial potential, for executives who want to see their
companies grow, and for all those concerned with business
ideas and management education.

'Rosabeth Kanter is a sociologist who has a remarkable track
record. Each of her previous books addressed a 'hot' issue of the
day and stood out as 'the' book – one that would last and
warrant re-reading long after the issue had faded from the
media. With *The Change Masters* Rosabeth Kanter has added
another book to that enviable record.'
                                           Sloan Management Review

'... a narrative about success, culminating in how to be an
effective change master, "adept at the art of anticipating the
need for, and of leading, productive change". It builds upon
some very readable cases of companies which adapt readily and
successfully to new working practices, enterprises and perspec-
tives on their worlds.'   *Times Higher Education Supplement*

CREATING EXCELLENCE: *Managing Corporate Culture, Strategy and Change in the New Age*
Craig Hickman and Michael A. Silva

Based on a programme of six essential leadership skills – vision, sensitivity, insight, versatility, focus and patience – this step-by-step blueprint for organisational excellence shows the New Age Executive exactly how to:

- know your firm's capabilities – and make the most of them
- motivate your people to peak performance
- respond positively to change from within and without
- develop long-term goals and see them through
- and turn *crisis* into *opportunity*

All these principles are illustrated with fascinating case studies of the most spectacular successes and failures in the recent history of American enterprise, from the rise of K Mart to the demise of Osborne Computers. In addition, hands-on 'exercises' will enable you to test their application to the concerns of your own organisation.

Whether you work for a small business or a vast conglomerate, in a hot new industry or a mature, stable environment, *Creating Excellence* can help make you the most important corporate asset of the eighties – and beyond.

'This book is crisp, intelligent and stimulating. It analyses perceptively the essential qualities of the successful business and business leader. The authors are both practising businessmen, and they add concrete detail to their concepts, as well as drawing on empirical business experience in the US. The result is a refreshingly substantial and very readable study.'
Financial Mail

'Business people with ties to both the new and the old will profit from the forward looking counsel of these management consultants. This worthy addition to a popular genre is a cogent and assimilable review of well-founded management practices.' *The American Library Association Book List*

'laudable ... useful and integrative ideas to ponder.'
Management Review

THE RISK TAKERS
Portraits of Money, Ego and Power
Jeffrey Robinson

This extremely upbeat, highly readable yet deadly serious look at the City's 'high flyers' is for anyone interested in big business, and everyone interested in the personalities who make the headlines. THE RISK TAKERS lifts the men who make those headlines off the front page and puts them under the microscope to reveal for the very first time in depth, just what makes them tick.

'Jeffrey Robinson's forthright and sardonic study of the financial power wielders among Britain's entrepreneurs has deadly serious value as well as being a vividly entertaining book.'
Lloyds List

'Robinson makes some pleasingly astringent comments on his risk-takers, whom he is far from viewing with starry eyes.'
Times Literary Supplement

'The Risk Takers as entrepreneurs are the pirates, the merchant adventurers, the soldiers of fortune of this age and generation. The author has chosen his characters well, and they are mostly 'characters'. This book gives you an insight into what makes these people tick, and you can play them and judge them. Read this book and go and be a player, not a spectator.'
Sir Kenneth Cork, Accountancy

SECRET MONEY
Ingo Walter

International financial secrecy has attracted major interest in recent years as a number of important money laundering, tax evasion, fraud and bribery cases have made the headlines, and as capital has fled from countries caught up in the international financial crises of the 1980s. This major new book, the first of its kind, lays bare the secrets of this secret world and will be required reading for all those fascinated by this most mysterious and important aspect of international finance and business.

'his book is a gripping and impeccably researched international drama ... tax evasion, laundering of "dirty" money and other moves in this market all add up to colossal movements in capital. The first thorough, professional and detached examination of this market and the commodity in which it deals – secret money.'   *Lloyds List*

'*Secret Money* is a worthy Baedeker to the dark side of the world of finance. Walter provides a concise set of thumb-nail studies of major scandals from the Bank of Boston's cash laundromat to the Panamanian black hole down which Calvi's Banco Ambrosiano poured roughly $1.4 billion. That alone makes *Secret Money* a good reference source. Here and there, too, giant flashes of mordant wit. A must read for tax cheats, con artists, drug backers and cops.'   *Institutional Investor*

THE ZURICH AXIOMS
Max Gunther

The Zurich Axioms is a term coined some years ago by a group of enterprising Swiss speculators in Wall Street who wanted to get rich, and refers to the remarkably simple, innovative and extremely effective set of principles they evolved about the handling of investment and risk. The most inexperienced investor can use the Axioms successfully, provided he or she is willing to accept the basic premise that, in finance as in anything else, 'nothing venture, nothing gain' is a law against which there is no appeal. If you want to get rich, you must learn neither to avoid risk nor to court it foolhardily, but to *manage* it – and enjoy it, too.

CHAOS IS NOT DANGEROUS UNTIL IT STARTS TO LOOK ORDERLY

'Max Gunther's twelve major and sixteen minor axioms are actually a lucid and powerful presentation of one leading school of thought's conclusions about how to operate in the financial markets. Basically, this school argues that you must speculate to accumulate. Risk is to the investor what battle is to the general.

Gunther explicitly recognizes the importance of emotional self-knowledge. And where speculation is compulsory, Gunther's axioms seem prudent indeed.'

The Times Literary Supplement

WHEN THE SHIP STARTS TO SINK, DON'T PRAY. JUMP.

'Good old home truths about the business of speculation. As Max Gunther breezily admits, they apply just as much to poker as to the Stock Exchange. In the end he argues "All investment is speculation, the only difference is some people admit it and some do not."'

The Financial Times

Other Business Books available in Unwin Paperbacks:

The Change Masters: Corporate Entrepreneurs at Work   £4.95 ☐
Rosabeth Moss Kanter
Cheats at Work   £3.95 ☐
Gerald Mars
Creating Excellence: Managing Corporate Culture, Strategy and
Change in the New Age   £3.95 ☐
Craig Hickman and Michael A Silva
Pay-off: Wheeling and Dealing in the Arab World   £2.95 ☐
Said K Aburish
The Risk Takers: Portraits of Money, Ego and Power   £2.95 ☐
Jeffrey Robinson
Secret Money   £4.95 ☐
Ingo Walter
Silicon Valley Fever: Growth of High Technology Culture   £4.95 ☐
Judith K Larsen and Everett M Rogers
Strategies for Women at Work   £4.95 ☐
Janice LaRouche and Regina Ryan
The Zurich Axioms   £2.95 ☐
Max Gunther

All these books are available at your local bookshop or newsagent, or can be ordered direct by post. Just tick the titles you want and fill in the form below.

Name ....

Address ....

....

....

Write to Unwin Cash Sales, PO Box 11, Falmouth, Cornwall TR10 9EN.

Please enclose remittance to the value of the cover price plus:

UK: 60p for the first book plus 25p for the second book, thereafter 15p for each additional book ordered to a maximum charge of £1.90.

BFPO and EIRE: 60p for the first book plus 25p for the second book and 15p for the next 7 books and thereafter 9p per book.

OVERSEAS INCLUDING EIRE: £1.25 for the first book plus 75p for the second book and 28p for each additional book.

Unwin Paperbacks reserve the right to show new retail prices on covers, which may differ from those previously advertised in the text or elsewhere. Postage rates are also subject to revision.